T0323816

# Single-Session Therapy

The new edition of *Single-Session Therapy: Distinctive Features* provides an up-to-date general introduction to the field of Single-Session Therapy (SST).

Written by eminent clinician and author Windy Dryden, this book challenges mainstream therapeutic assumptions, predicated on the certainty that clients will have more than one therapy session. Following the popular Distinctive Features format, the book is divided into two sections, with 15 chapters describing theoretical features and 15 offering practical techniques of SST. Updates to the revised edition include new chapters on the importance of the working alliance in SST, on different types of help that clients seek from SST and on common errors in SST and how to avoid them.

*Single-Session Therapy* will be of interest to those across the psychotherapy and counselling professions and will provide extensive guidance for students, trainees and practitioners alike.

**Windy Dryden** is in clinical and consultative practice and is an international authority on Single-Session Therapy. He is Emeritus Professor of Psychotherapeutic Studies at Goldsmiths, University of London. He has worked in psychotherapy for more than 45 years and is the author or editor of over 265 books.

# Psychotherapy and Counselling Distinctive Features

The Psychotherapy and Counselling Distinctive Features series provides readers with an introduction to the distinctive theoretical and practical features of various therapeutic approaches from leading practitioners in their field.

Each book in this series focuses on one particular approach and guides the reader through 30 features – both theoretical and practical – that are particularly distinctive of that approach. Written for practitioners by practitioners, this series will also be of interest to trainees, social workers and many others outside the therapeutic tradition.

Series Editor: Windy Dryden

## Titles in the series:

### Single-Session Therapy
*Windy Dryden*

### Single-Session Therapy Second Edition
*Windy Dryden*

For further information about this series please visit: https://www.routledge.com/Psychotherapy-and-Counselling-Distinctive-Features/book-series/PCDF

# Single-Session Therapy

## Distinctive Features
Second Edition

# Windy Dryden

Routledge
Taylor & Francis Group

LONDON AND NEW YORK

Designed cover image: © Getty Images

Second edition published 2024
by Routledge
4 Park Square, Milton Park, Abingdon, Oxon, OX14 4RN

and by Routledge
605 Third Avenue, New York, NY 10158

*Routledge is an imprint of the Taylor & Francis Group, an informa business*

© 2024 Windy Dryden

First edition published by Routledge 2019

*British Library Cataloguing-in-Publication Data*
A catalogue record for this book is available from the British Library

*Library of Congress Cataloging-in-Publication Data*
Names: Dryden, Windy, author.
Title: Single-session therapy: distinctive features / Windy Dryden.
Description: Second edition. |
Milton Park, Abingdon, Oxon ; New York, NY :
Routledge, 2024. | Series: Psychotherapy and
counselling distinctive features |
Includes bibliographical references and index.
Identifiers: LCCN 2023020812 (print) |
LCCN 2023020813 (ebook) | ISBN 9781032536781 (hardback) |
ISBN 9781032535852 (paperback) | ISBN 9781003413103 (ebook)
Subjects: LCSH: Single-session psychotherapy.
Classification: LCC RC480.55.D77 2024 (print) |
LCC RC480.55 (ebook) |
DDC 616.89/14–dc23/eng/20230710
LC record available at https://lccn.loc.gov/2023020812
LC ebook record available at https://lccn.loc.gov/2023020813

ISBN: 9781032536781 (hbk)
ISBN: 9781032535852 (pbk)
ISBN: 9781003413103 (ebk)

DOI: 10.4324/9781003413103

Typeset in Times New Roman
by Newgen Publishing UK

# Contents

# Preface

Single-Session Therapy (SST) is not new. Sigmund Freud, the father of psychoanalysis (hardly a brief therapy), was reported to have carried out two well-known single-session treatments with Aurelia Öhm-Kronich ('Katharina') in 1893 (Freud & Breuer, 1895) and with the famous composer, Gustav Mahler, in 1910 (Kuehn, 1965). Alfred Adler, who split from Freud to develop what eventually became known as Adlerian Therapy, established a number of child guidance clinics in the 1920s where he would do single-session demonstrations of his technique with parents and children, separately and together, in front of a mixed professional and lay audience. For 40 years (from 1965 to 2005), Albert Ellis did SST with volunteer members of a largely lay audience at the Institute that bore his name (Ellis & Joffe, 2002). Most of Milton Erickson's known cases lasted for a single session (O'Hanlon & Hexum, 1990) and the famous 'Gloria' films where 'Gloria' was interviewed by Carl Rogers, Fritz Perls and Albert Ellis in 1965 can be seen as SSTs.

To some degree, SST lost its way in the 1970s and early 1980s despite important work by Bernard Bloom (1981). It was not until the early 1990s when Moshe Talmon (1990) published his seminal book entitled *Single-Session Therapy: Maximising the Effect of the First (and Often Only) Therapeutic Encounter*, reporting on work carried out at the Kaiser Permanente Clinic in California with his colleagues Michael Hoyt and Robert Rosenbaum, that interest was rekindled in SST.

Since then and increasingly since 2012 (when the first international symposium took place), SST has attracted much attention as the world grapples to offer therapeutic help at the point of need rather than at the point of availability. These developments can be seen in the edited books that were published from three international symposia that took place in Australia (twice) and Canada[1] (Hoyt & Talmon, 2014a; Hoyt, Bobele, Slive, Young & Talmon, 2018a; and Hoyt, Young & Rycroft, 2021).

Training in psychotherapy and counselling is still predicated on the idea that clients will certainly have more than one session. This is the case even though, worldwide, the most frequent number of sessions people have is 'one' (Hoyt & Talmon, 2014b). This 'wake-up' call provides the backdrop for this book.

As with other books in the 'Psychotherapy and Counselling Distinctive Features' series, this volume is divided into two parts: theory and practice, with 15 distinctive features discussed in each part. Unlike other books in the series, *Single-Session Therapy* is not an approach. Rather, as you will see, it is a mindset that underpins a way of working that practitioners from diverse approaches can adopt. The SST community is a broad church with therapists working with individuals, couples and groups (Hoyt & Talmon, 2014a; Hoyt et al., 2018a; and Hoyt, Young & Rycroft, 2021). My own SST practice is with individuals and, although I have tried to write a book that people from the SST community would think is fair-minded, I do have my biases. When I have drawn upon my own experience, I have tried to make this clear. Having said that, this book is far more general in scope than a book I wrote for my 'CBT Distinctive Features' series (Dryden, 2022a) entitled

---

1 The fourth international symposium on SST will take place in Italy in November 2023.

*Single-Session Integrated Cognitive Behaviour Therapy (SSI-CBT): Distinctive Features.*

Please be aware that this current book is likely to challenge mainstream therapeutic beliefs. I hope that you will read it with an open mind. If you do, it might change your practice for the better.

# Part 1

# Theory

# Chapter 1

# What's in a Name

## Abstract

In this opening chapter, I consider the nature of single-session therapy (SST) by discussing some of the names that it has been given.

## Single-Session Therapy (SST)

If one considers the name, 'single-session therapy', and takes it literally, its meaning seems clear. It means a therapy that lasts for a single session. While a few people in the field may see it this way, most contemporary SST therapists disagree with this view as we shall presently see.

### Talmon's (1990) definition

One of the pioneers of SST, Moshe Talmon (1990) provided the following definition in his seminal book. He said, 'Single-session therapy is defined here as one face-to-face meeting between a therapist and a patient with no previous or subsequent sessions within one year' (Talmon, 1990: xv). This means that the therapist and client could have non-face-to-face meetings and the therapy could still be regarded as SST.

DOI: 10.4324/9781003413103-2

### *Hoyt et al.'s (2018b) refinement*

Hoyt, Bobele, Slive, Young & Talmon (2018b) distanced themselves from Talmon's (1990) definition, which they say was used for research purposes. They argue that the point that there should be no other sessions in the year before or after was arbitrary and the 'face-to-face' criterion predated the development of online communication platforms such as Zoom. They make the point that the work discussed in Talmon's book was based on the fact that many people attend only one session and, consequently, therapist and client are advised to approach the first session *as if* it were going to be the last. Twenty-eight years after the publication of Talmon's book, Hoyt et al. (2018b: 18, footnote) said the following: 'SST clients may be seen more than once in a year (nowadays either face-to-face or via telephone or online), and the basic SST desideratum is that a session be approached as though it could be the only (single) session, complete unto itself'. However, as most SST theorists and therapists now stress, if a client needs further sessions they should be made available to the person. This more nuanced view where the session is treated as if it were to be the only session, but that further sessions are available if requested by the client, is perhaps the most dominant in the field of SST today.

### One-at-a-Time (OAAT) Therapy, SST and the Enforced Waiting Period

Michael Hoyt (2011) introduced the term 'One-at-a-Time Therapy' to the literature. This term has been accepted by the SST community as shown by its inclusion in the title of Hoyt et al.'s (2018a) book, '*Single-Session Therapy by Walk-In[1] or Appointment: Administrative, Clinical, and Supervisory Aspects of One-at-a-Time Services*'. As the term suggests,

---

1 Because some clients are not physically able to 'walk in', this term is now falling out of favour. In its stead, I use the term 'open-access, enter now'.

'One-at-a-Time' Therapy (OAATT) is a therapy that occurs one session at a time. The client is informed that one session of therapy may suffice, but, if not, they can book another session. What they cannot do is to book a series of sessions.

In the United Kingdom, many university and college counselling services who offer SST services refer to these services as OAATT and some have organised their therapy delivery service so that student clients who want further help can only access a second single session two weeks after they have had their first session. This means that students do not have the option of accessing further help immediately after their first session and this, in my view, is an unnecessary obstacle to the person getting help at the point of their determined need. It is more in keeping with what the administration considers it can offer its clients.

OAATT fits with what Nicholas Cummings (1990) called brief intermittent psychotherapy through the life cycle. Here, a person would seek therapy when they had a problem that they could not solve by themself. They would leave therapy when they felt able to address the problem independently. The OAATT framework allows the person to address their problem one session at a time, to come and go, as it were, and return whenever they feel that they could benefit from therapy, except where the two-week waiting period has been introduced.

This enforced waiting period is not only used in OAATT services. It is also used by agencies who offer SST and who say to clients that the agency will contact them two or three weeks after their first session to see how they are getting along and whether they need further help. Again the problem here is that the client does not have the option of requesting help at the end of their first SST session. Such agencies who have an enforced waiting period do so because they want clients to reflect on the session that they have had, digest what they have learned, put such learning into practice and then let things settle before deciding whether or not to book another session (see Chapter 29).

## ONEplus Therapy

We have seen that the term 'single-session therapy' (SST) has its difficulties since, no matter how many times it is explained to people that it does not mean that clients cannot access further help, if needed, they still think of it as 'one-off-therapy', where clients are only offered a single session of therapy. Young (2018) is aware of this phenomenon but has argued that we retain SST as the dominant term since it has a 'shock value' and it creates an interest in therapists who want to find out what SST is. I can understand this, but, as one of the most important aspects of the single-session mindset is clarity, I think we should be clear about the mode of therapy delivery we are proposing by making it clear in what we call it.

We have also seen that the term 'One-at-a-Time Therapy' (OAATT) has its problems, particularly where the way it is offered appears to conflict with the principle of 'help at the point of need', which is so central to this form of work (see Chapter 4).

For these reasons, I use the term ONEplus therapy to describe the way I work in this domain. As you will see, the 'ONE' in ONEplus therapy is in capitals and emphasises that the intention in this form of work is to join with the client to help them take away from the session their stated wants. The 'plus' in ONEplus therapy is joined to the word 'ONE' to indicate that if the client wants more help at the end of the session, they can have it (within the confines of what services the therapist or the agency offer). Also, the word 'plus' does not specify when the person can or cannot request extra help. Let me reiterate, if the client wants another session, for example, at the end of the first session. they can have it.

While I have made clear why I favour the term ONEplus therapy, I am fully aware that this is a personal view and is not (yet) accepted in the SST field. For this reason, in this book,

I will continue to refer to the therapy delivery mode in question as 'Single-Session Therapy' which I define as follows:

Single-Session Therapy (SST) is an intentional form of therapy delivery where the therapist and client contract to meet for a session of therapy and work together to help the client to achieve their stated wants from that session on the understanding that further help is available to the client on request.

## SST by Design and SST by Default

It is important to distinguish between SST by design and SST by default. SST by design occurs when the therapist and client intentionally embark on single-session therapy (as shown in the definition above). This could be a single session with no prospect of further sessions or one where one or more sessions are possible. The critical point is that both the therapist and client agree on this before embarking on therapy.

SST by default occurs when a client attends one session when both therapist and client anticipate that therapy would involve a longer-term contract. Here, the client has decided not to attend another session. In this case, they may cancel the next scheduled appointment or not turn up for it. Therapists often refer to clients who do not return for a second session as 'drop-outs' from treatment, mainly if a client does not show up for an appointment that they have not cancelled. In short, SST by default tends to be seen as the client dropping out of therapy, and this is generally viewed negatively by therapists who think that the client has derived little or no benefit from the session that they had. Actually, and surprisingly perhaps, when SST is by default most clients are satisfied with the session that they have had and consider that they have received the help that they were looking for (Hoyt et al., 2018b; Talmon, 1990).

## SST by Appointment or by Open-Access, Enter Now

Finally, SST may occur by appointment or by open-access, enter now. In the former, the person learns about the SST service and contacts the service to make an appointment with a therapist. In the latter, the person literally accesses the service, without an appointment, completes a short intake form and usually sees a therapist immediately or after a short break. While further sessions are available in both 'by appointment' and 'open-access', enter now settings, the nature of the latter means that often people do not return for further therapy.

# Chapter 2

# Misconceptions about SST

## Abstract

In the last chapter, I considered the nature of SST by discussing some of the terms that have been used when describing this way of working. In this chapter, I look at further defining the field by considering nine misconceptions that are held by some when they are first introduced to SST and by others even before they have been introduced to it! Having listed each misconception, I set out to correct it.

## SST Is a Therapeutic Orientation or a Single Way of Working

In Chapter 5, I introduce the view that perhaps the best way of thinking about SST is to consider it to involve a mindset, a particular way of viewing the work that influences practice. Consequently, SST is not a therapeutic orientation in the same way as couples therapy is not a therapeutic orientation. Also, like couples therapy, SST does not involve a single way of working. Although perhaps the dominant ideas on SST have come from what I have called the 'constructive' approaches (including solution-focused therapy, collaborative therapy, narrative therapy and strengths-based therapy), SST can and has been practised by therapists from a range of other orientations (Dryden, 2024). Suffice it to say there is no one approach to

DOI: 10.4324/9781003413103-3

SST. It is a mindset and a way of delivering therapeutic services that is based on that mindset.

## SST Is a 'Cure-All'

Advocates of SST are keen to make clear that SST is best seen as occupying an important place in a range of therapy services available within an agency's therapy provision. It is not supposed to replace such services, and nobody in the SST community would recommend that it does so. If, at the end of the session, a client wants to access more help, they can do so, as long as the agency (in this case) offers that help. So, it is perfectly possible for a client to have a single session, realise at the end of the session that they would benefit from longer-term therapy, make this clear and have their therapy preferences met as long as the agency offers longer-term work.

## SST Is a Quick Fix

The term 'quick fix' means something that seems to be a fast and easy solution to a problem but is, in fact, not very good or will not last long. This is not what SST therapists attempt to do. Instead, they strive to work with clients to find a meaningful, durable solution to a problem or to help them take steps that will lead to such a solution.

## SST Is Used to Save Money and Reduce Waiting Lists

Budget holders may be attracted to SST because they see it as a way of reducing costs. In Chapter 4, I argue that SST is based on the idea that help should be provided at the point of need rather than at the point of availability. When services are restructured to provide 'at the point of need' help then it may be that money is also saved. Even if this the case, this should not be the prime reason for this way of delivering therapeutic services.

SST has a therapeutic *intention*, which is to help the person, if possible, take away from the session something that will help solve their nominated problem. When introduced into an agency it has the *consequence* of reducing waiting lists and waiting times. In SST we would argue that the above *intention* should ideally be the reason why SST is offered and not the above *consequence*.

## SST Restricts Access to Therapy

The basic idea behind SST is not to offer clients only one session but to help them get the most out of the session on the basis that it *may* be the only session that they have. It is possible to offer clients one session of therapy that is not informed by the principle of helping them get the most out of the session. To my mind, this would be the worst of both worlds – restricting the client to one session and not helping them to get the most out of the session.

In most SST services, further sessions are possible, either booked at the end of the session or after a waiting period where the client reflects on what they learned from the session, digests this learning, acts on it and sees if they need further help.

Thus, SST does not restrict access to therapy. Instead, it is tempered by the needs of all who use the service so that nobody has to wait longer than they need to.

## SST Is Speeded-Up Therapy

Some people think that SST is like 'therapy speeded up' where the therapist attempts to cram a number of sessions into one session. This is not the case. In fact, if a therapist attempts to do this, it often renders SST ineffective. SST is guided by two principles: 'sooner is better' and 'less is more'. When I first started to practise SST, my tendency was to give the client as much as possible to take away with them, but I soon learned that this meant that the person takes nothing away with them.

As Michael Hoyt has stressed for years and again recently (Hoyt, 2018), a single session has its own process. It does not try to truncate the process of, for example, a six-session therapy into one session. The session is regarded as a whole to be complete in itself (Talmon, 1990).

## SST Is the Same as Crisis Intervention

While a single session can help people with crises, SST is not the same as crisis intervention. Thus, a person does not have to be in crisis to benefit from SST. Also, a person in crisis may need a number of sessions to resolve the crisis.

## SST Is Easy Because It Involves One Session

Some therapists think that long-term therapy is complex and this may be the case. These therapists think that, by contrast, brief therapy is relatively easy and, by extension, SST is the easiest of them all. However, I would beg to differ. If 'less is more' in SST (see above), 'less is also more difficult'. Given its brevity and focus, SST is quite difficult to practise, and therapists who practise it require high-level therapeutic skills.

## SST Is for Everyone

While SST can be helpful, it is certainly not for all clients. There are clients who want ongoing therapy – whether they need it or not – and these people would not respond well to being offered a single session even if further sessions may be available and even if a compelling rationale for its use has been made. Other clients want the security of an ongoing relationship with a therapist, and their clinical preferences should be respected (Norcross & Cooper, 2021).

Also, SST is not for all therapists. Some therapists believe that they can only practise therapy once they have carried out a full history and case formulation. Clearly, this cannot be done in SST, and such therapists would struggle to practise when time is at a premium.

It is neither a good idea to require clients to have SST when it is not wanted, nor to mandate therapists to practise SST, particularly where their ideas and related skills are not consistent with the SST mindset (see Chapter 5). On the contrary, SST is best practised when clients see the potential in it, and therapists embrace the challenge of helping willing clients in the shortest possible period. For a fuller treatment of such misconceptions about SST, see Dryden (2022b).

Chapter 3

# People Have the Capacity to Help Themselves Quickly

## Abstract

Single-session therapy rests on the assumption that people can help themselves quickly if the conditions are in place for them to do so. If this were not the case, then SST would not be possible. In this chapter, I present an example of how someone helped themself quickly and then use this example to spell out the four significant conditions that need to be in place for someone to help themself quickly.

## The Case of Paul and His Fear of Heights

I got a call from Paul who discovered that I offer SST among my clinical services. He wanted to propose to his girlfriend Angela in a romantic setting, and her sister told him in confidence that it was Angela's dream to be proposed to at the top of the Eiffel Tower. This posed a problem for Paul since he had a longstanding fear of heights. He had arranged for himself and Angela to go to Paris in five days' time and was keen to propose to her during the trip in a surprise visit to the Eiffel Tower. Could I, he enquired, help him to overcome his fear of heights without using hypnosis, which he had tried before, and which did not suit him. I replied that while this was a 'tall' order, if we both gave it our best shot, we would see if we could solve the

DOI: 10.4324/9781003413103-4

problem. He agreed, and we decided to meet for a single session the next day.

At the session, it transpired that Paul was anxious about the swaying sensations he predicted he would get when in high places, along with the image of him throwing himself off wherever he was. As we explored a little further, Paul confirmed that the swaying sensations were evidence to him that he was losing control, something that he held that he could not tolerate. I asked Paul if he would like to hear my view of why he had the images of throwing himself off the high space, and he was keen to hear them. My view was that these images stemmed from Paul's intolerant attitude towards the swaying sensations and if he tolerated these sensations without liking them, then eventually they would not linger in his mind for long. Paul agreed with this view and was keen to apply what we then discussed. This was that he needed to expose himself to his swaying sensations, first on the ground and then in high places. Paul resolved to do this and spent the next two days doing so. He texted the next week telling me that he proposed to Angela at the top of the Eiffel Tower and she accepted!

## The Four Conditions of Rapid Change

In my view, for a person to help themself quickly, four conditions need to be present: (i) knowledge; (ii) a committed reason to change; (iii) preparedness to accept the costs of change, if any; and (iv) taking appropriate action. As we shall see, all four conditions' ingredients were present in Paul's case, and therefore he was able to change in a short period.

### Knowledge

Knowing what to do is probably the weakest of the four conditions in accounting for rapid change. In some approaches to SST (e.g. CBT-based approaches), knowledge is crucial, while, in other approaches, it is relatively unimportant and may be counterproductive (e.g. Ericksonian approaches).

For Paul, however, knowledge was significant in two respects. First, knowledge helped him to make sense of why he was having the symptoms that he was experiencing and, second, it showed him what he needed to do to address his problem adequately. If you do not know what to do, then you will not do it, but knowing what to do does not mean that you are going to do it. This is why knowledge can be a key condition in facilitating rapid change but is usually insufficient.

### A Committed Reason to Change

Having a good reason to change and being committed to the reason is core. The timeliness of the change is a central factor here too. Thus, Paul wanted to address his fear of heights, not for himself, but for his girlfriend who had always dreamed of receiving a proposal of marriage at the top of the Eiffel Tower. The time factor was that they were both going to Paris five days after he made contact with me. If he was going to propose, he had to take action promptly.

### Preparedness to Accept Any Costs of Change

Unfortunately, psychological change usually involves the person experiencing some costs. These costs may be internal (e.g. the person has to put up with some pain or discomfort to get the desired benefit), interpersonal (e.g. some of the person's relationships may suffer if they make the change) or pragmatic (the person may lose specific benefits if they change). If the person is prepared to accept such costs, they will tend to change; if not, they will not change. Paul had to accept internal costs if he was to address his fear of heights effectively. These costs were that he would need to tolerate the discomfort of his swaying sensations and the images of him throwing himself from high places while facing these places. Paul stated that he was prepared to accept these costs of change.

### Taking Appropriate Action

A person may meet the previous three criteria, but, unless they are prepared to take action based on what they have learned when discussing these conditions with their therapist, they probably won't change. Paul knew that to achieve his goal of proposing to Angela at the top of the Eiffel Tower, he needed first to seek out a number of high places and tolerate the swaying sensations and the images of him throwing himself off each place. He did this and only left each place when he was no longer afraid. As a result, Paul was able to go to the top of the Eiffel Tower without anxiety and proposed to Angela, a proposal which she accepted.

It is incredible sometimes what people can achieve in a very short period. Rod Temperton, the British songwriter from Cleethorpes who wrote 'Thriller' for Michael Jackson, decided with Quincy Jones, the producer, that he would write verses to be read by Vincent Price at the end of the song. Price was coming to the studio the next day at 2 pm, so Temperton gave himself six hours to do the writing and deliver it to the studio. However, he had forgotten that his British agent was coming to have a breakfast meeting, which lasted until noon that day. Temperton now had two hours to write the verses and deliver them. He did so with moments to spare and the results, as anyone familiar with 'Thriller' would know, were spectacular (Pitman, 2017).

Chapter 4

# SST Is Based on Providing Help at the Point of Need

## (Rather Than Help at the Point of Availability)

### Abstract

In this chapter, I compare two pathways to help, one based on providing help at the point of need and the other based on providing help at the point of availability. In looking at the assumptions underlying each pathway, it is clear that SST is based on providing help at the point of need.

### Introduction

The idea of SST can often be tangled up in the minds of professionals with notions such as 'quick fix', 'flight into health', 'spontaneous remission', 'treatment dropout' and 'superficial change'. With such pejorative ideas associated with SST, it is often hard for SST therapists to get a fair hearing when presenting SST to colleagues who are not already advocates of this way of working. However, when we look at what clients say about SST services, a very different picture emerges.

### Pathways to Help

If you ask clients to choose between having a single session of therapy with the promise of at least another session if needed or having ongoing therapy, probably most would choose the latter. However, if the choice was the same but put into a more realistic

DOI: 10.4324/9781003413103-5

context, then a different answer may be forthcoming. Thus, if the question was 'Which pathway would you like to opt for, pathway 1 or pathway 2? In pathway 1, you would have a single session of therapy immediately (or with only a few days' wait) with at least another session if you needed it. In pathway 2, you would be put onto a waiting list for an assessment for ongoing therapy, and if deemed suitable you would be put onto another waiting list for actual treatment with a combined waiting time of a number of months', I guess that a significant number would opt for pathway 1.

## An Example of Pathway 1

This was indeed the case at a UK university that had been using a six-session counselling model where all students were offered a maximum of six counselling sessions before realising that they could not sustain this service delivery in the face of growing and unsustainable waiting lists. This six-session contract was itself a reduction from the previous 12-session contract! They had decided that they wanted to initiate some kind of SST service delivery when they sought my consultancy and training help. Eventually, they settled on what I would classify as an OAATT service delivery approach, which they introduced at the beginning of the next academic year. Here, students would be seen quickly and they could book another session at the end of the first, but they could not book a series of appointments. This resulted in a slashing of the waiting list, which at the service's busiest point was only five days as compared to the many weeks' wait for an appointment when the six-session contract was in place.

Interestingly, when student opinion was canvassed, students who began their college course at the same time as the OAAT service was introduced were most appreciative of being able to have a counselling session when they needed it. By contrast, returning students who were accustomed to the six-session model complained about losing services. This shows the importance of placing SST in context when introducing it to service users and other professionals.

The voice of new students at the university clearly indicated the importance of help being provided at the point of need rather than at the point of availability.

## Help at the Point of Need

Nobody in the helping professions would argue with the ideal that all people who require psychological assistance should be offered the help they need at the point of that need. The problem is that we live in a world of scarce resources, and it is very unlikely that financial budgets will ever be provided to enable this to happen, especially in a National Health Service such as exists in the United Kingdom today. Consequently, decisions must be made concerning how to structure services to improve access to psychological therapies. Of course, such decisions are often driven by budgetary concerns, but not exclusively. These decisions are also informed by what people believe is central to providing help to clients. In Table 4.1, I have outlined some assumptions that underly the two different ways of structuring psychological services: providing help at the point of need and at the point of availability.

As you will see from this table, the assumptions that underlie help provided at the point of need stress the importance of responding when the person seeks help, and to provide therapy from the outset rather than other services that do not involve active treatment.

I made the point at the beginning of the chapter that therapists new to SST are often sceptical about what can be achieved from a single session. However, when service users are followed-up and asked about their experiences of SST, the majority indicate that they are satisfied with the help provided (see Hoyt & Talmon, 2014b).

*Table 4.1*  Help provided at the point of need versus at the point of availability: some underlying assumptions

| Help Provided at the Point of Need | Help Provided at the Point of Availability |
|---|---|
| • It is better to respond to client need by providing some help straightaway rather than by waiting to provide the best possible help, unless the person chooses to wait for the latter | • It is better to have clients wait for the best possible help than to provide them with some help when they need it |
| • Providing immediate help is more important than carrying out an assessment | • Carrying out an assessment is more important than offering immediate help |
| • Therapy should start immediately. A case formulation should be carried out, if needed | • Therapy should only be carried out on the basis of a formulation of the case |
| • Therapy can be initiated in the absence of a case history | • It is important to take a case history before therapy is initiated |
| • People have the resources to make use of help provided at the point of need | • People have the resources to make use of help provided on the basis of a case formulation |
| • Sooner is better | • More is better |
| • The best way to see if a client will respond well to therapy is by offering them therapy and seeing how they respond | • The best way to see if a client will respond well to therapy is to offer them the most appropriate therapy based on a full assessment of their problems and on a formulation of their 'case' |

*(Continued)*

*Table 4.1* (Continued)

| Help Provided at the Point of Need | Help Provided at the Point of Availability |
| --- | --- |
| • Therapy can be initiated and risk managed if this becomes an issue | • Risk has to be properly managed before therapy is initiated |
| • Appropriate therapy length is best determined by the client | • Appropriate therapy length is best determined by the therapist |
| • When a person does not return for another session this may well indicate that the person is satisfied with what they achieved, although it may be the case that they were dissatisfied with the help provided | • When a person does not return for another session or before they have completed their 'course of treatment', they have dropped out of this treatment and it should be regarded as a bad outcome |

Chapter 5

# The SST Mindset

## Abstract

In this chapter, I consider and discuss the components of what is called the therapist's SST mindset. I will also outline what I consider to be the client's SST mindset. If the client is to get the most out of the single session, it is crucial for the therapist and client to have SST mindsets that are compatible.

## The Therapist's Mindset in SST

While there are some core practices within SST that I will discuss in more detail in the second part of this book, it is constructive to consider what some in the SST community describe as the single-session mindset. An excellent overview of this mindset is provided by Jeff Young (2018: 44), which he calls an 'SST informed attitude to clinical work'. It is important to make clear at the outset that Young's SST mindset is held in the minds of therapists. Later, I will consider what might comprise a client-held SST mindset. From a working alliance perspective (see Chapter 13), unless both therapist and client approach SST with a similar mindset, the latter will not get as much as they could from the work than if they do share this mindset. Indeed, the work may not even commence.

DOI: 10.4324/9781003413103-6

### Move Forward on the 'as-if' Principle

As I discussed in Chapter 1, there is no universally agreed definition of SST. However, there is what I call the 'as-if' principle to which the majority of SST therapists would adhere. This describes the phenomenon where therapists approach the first session 'as if' it could be the only session they have with a client. This is the case, says Young (2018: 44), 'irrespective of diagnosis, complexity or severity'. That being said, this mindset includes the idea that further help is possible should the client request it.

### Develop an End-of-Session Focus

Instead of asking the client what they want to achieve by the end of *therapy*, the SST therapist, mindful that this may be the only session that they have with the client (see above), has it in mind to ask the client what they would like to achieve by the end of the *session*. This focuses the client's mind on the now rather than some unspecified time in the perhaps far-off future when therapy might end.

### Agree on a Focus for the Session

Once the client has specified what they would like to leave with at the end of the session, the SST therapist negotiates a focus for the session with the client that will help them achieve their goal.

### Keep on Track

Given that time is at a premium in SST and given the human tendency to drift away from an agreed focus, the therapist keeps it in mind that it is their responsibility to keep the client on track, interrupting the client if necessary but always tactfully. My own suggestion is to ask clients at the outset for permission to interrupt them should the need arise.

### Utilise Client Strengths

All SST therapists agree that it is crucial to help clients to identify their strengths and apply them to the SST process both within the single session and to the application of learning after the session has ended.

### Share What Might Be Helpful

SST therapists draw upon a wealth of therapeutic wisdom from a plethora of different sources. Young (2018: 45) urges SST therapists to ask themselves, 'What would I want to share with this client if I never see them again?' While different therapists will have a different answer to this question, based in part on their favoured way of working, the critical point made by Young (2018) here is that any suggestions made should be put tentatively to the client for their consideration and discussion. Most SST therapists would also say that such suggestions should be based on effective strategies that the client has previously used on this and other issues, and should also make use of the client's strengths and resiliency factors.

### Utilise External Resources

Such resources may be other people in the client's life to whom they may turn for help or they may be online resources, geographically close organisational resources, support resources and booklets relevant to the client's concerns.

### Clarify Next Steps

It is generally agreed that, at the end of the session, the therapist and client should negotiate next steps. These steps may include the following: (i) the client concludes that they don't need further help because they have got what they came for; (ii) the client decides to go away to reflect on the session, digest what they learned, try out a few things on the basis of this learning, let things settle and book another session if one is required; (iii) the clients decides that they would like more help and discusses what is available with the therapist (see Chapter 29).

## The Client's Mindset in SST

Compared to the therapist's mindset in SST, there has been less written on what might be termed the client's mindset in SST. This describes the collection of ideas that clients hold about coming to therapy, which, if acted on, would help them gain as much as they could from the session. However, it is possible to extract such a mindset from writings on desirable client characteristics in SST (Dryden, 2022a; Talmon, 1990).

### Be Ready to Address the Problem Now

Some clients come to therapy with the idea that it will take them a long time to address their problems, with the result that it does. It is significant, therefore, for the client to have the idea that they may well be able to address their problem in one visit and be willing to join the therapist in an active alliance where both work hard together to do just that.

### Be Open to and Give Feedback on Any Suggestions from the Therapist

One of the components of the therapist's SST mindset, put forward by Young (2018), is the willingness to share something that the client may find helpful, but tentatively. If this can be received in an open-minded way by the client, who is then willing to voice any concerns about it rather than dismissing it out of hand or agreeing with it compliantly, then the resulting discussion can yield something perhaps more helpful than the therapist's original suggestion.

### Keep Expectations Realistic

As I will discuss in greater detail in the following chapter, it is vital for the client to have realistic expectations concerning what they can take from SST. The person who expects a profound shift in personality or quantum change (Miller & C' de Baca, 2001) after a single session is hoping for magic. Whereas, the person who hopes to get unstuck and take a few steps forward is demonstrating a realistic SST mindset.

### Be Prepared to Put Learning into Practice

When a client comes to a therapy session keen to put what they learn into practice, this mindset will encourage them to get the most from the session, especially if this commitment to action is ongoing.

When the client's and therapist's SST mindsets complement one another, they demonstrate a strong working alliance in the 'views' domain, which contributes to a good outcome from the session (Dryden, 2006, 2011).

# Chapter 6

# The Importance of Expectations in SST

## Abstract

In this chapter, I discuss the vital role that expectations play in SST. I begin by considering clients' expectations, particularly concerning the time therapy should take, but also about what can be achieved from a single session. I then discuss the expectations held by therapists and how they can shape and be shaped by clients' expectations.

## Clients' Expectations

In this section, I will discuss clients' expectations concerning time and outcome. Constantino, Ametrano & Greenberg (2012) distinguish between two types of client expectations in psychotherapy:

- *treatment expectations* (concerning what will happen during therapy), including how they and their therapists will behave (role expectations), their subjective experience of therapy (process expectations) and how long treatment will last (duration expectations)
- *outcome expectations* (concerning what they will achieve from therapy).

DOI: 10.4324/9781003413103-7

In this chapter, I will consider clients' duration expectations and outcome expectations.

## Duration Expectations

In an important chapter on time in brief therapy, Hoyt (1990: 115) makes the salient point that 'brief therapy is defined more by an attitude than by the specific number of treatment sessions'. This attitude can have a profound effect on both the therapist and the client. When considering the impact of clients' duration expectations, for example, Battino (2014) discusses hearing de Shazer (1982) talk about a research project carried out at the 'Brief Family Therapy Center' in Milwaukee on the effect of clients' expectations of the time therapy should take on their behaviour in therapy. In that study, clients were randomly told that therapists in that centre usually took either five or ten sessions to help people with their particular issue. What the researchers found was that clients in the 'five-session' treatment began doing 'significant' work in the fourth session and that clients in the 'ten-session treatment' began doing significant work in the eighth or ninth session. In commenting on this interesting finding, Battino (2014) cites the oft-quoted 'Parkinson's law of psychotherapy' (Appelbaum, 1975), which states that therapy expands and contracts to fill the time allocated to it.[1]

Thus, if clients expect therapy to last a specified period, this would determine the duration of therapy. Before I got interested in SST, occasionally an overseas client would wish to see me for a course of therapy while they were in London. On one occasion, I agreed to see the person for five sessions over a

---

1 This phenomenon also operates in other spheres of life. For example, I found as an academic that, if a deadline was set six months after a piece of work was given, most students would submit their work in the final 30 minutes of the deadline. However, if the same piece of work was due in nine months, again most students would submit their work in the final half-hour!

two-week period, and that proved to be helpful to the person. On another occasion, I had much less time to see another person and could only offer one session. The client accepted the offer, worked enormously hard in that session and achieved comparatively similar benefit to the person who had five sessions. I should add that restricting time in the second case was not a deliberate strategy so that the person would work hard in the very brief time they had with me. I genuinely only had one hour. It is only now when I look back at the two scenarios that I can see clearly that each client used the time allocated to them.

### Outcome Expectations

In Chapter 5, I mentioned that having realistic expectations for change was one of the features of what I called the client's SST mindset. If a client comes to therapy in a demoralised state thinking that nothing much can be achieved, the therapist needs to address this quickly and help the client to see that change, even from a single therapy session, is possible. Otherwise, a self-fulfilling prophecy may 'kick in' and yield little or no change for the client. Alternatively, if the client thinks that they will profoundly change their personality in a single session, then disappointment will usually ensue. However, if the client thinks that change is possible and that they can begin that process in one session with the therapist's help, this augurs well for a good outcome. The therapist helping the client to set realistic goals is usually a meaningful part of this process.

### Therapists' Expectations

Rosenthal & Jacobson (1968) carried out an important piece of research on the impact of teacher expectations on pupil performance. Children whose teachers expected them to achieve well did, in fact, achieve more than children whose teachers did not expect them to achieve well. This was the case despite there being no other differences between the two groups of children. This occurred through teachers responding to the 'intellectual bloomers', as the first group were called, in more positive ways than to children in the other group.

There is a vast literature on the impact of therapist expectations in psychotherapy (see Constantino, Glass, Arnkoff, Ametrano & Smith, 2011). In short, and extrapolating from Rosenthal & Jacobson's (1968) findings to therapy, if a therapist thinks that the client can gain from a single session, this will affect the therapist's behaviour in positive ways and lead to the client engaging more constructively with the process. Additionally, if the client thinks that they can gain from the single session, their behaviour will also have a galvanising impact on the therapist, who will then work harder to help the client achieve their goal.

As I said elsewhere:

> If both participants [in SST] expect change, then it is more likely to happen than if they don't. If the therapist expects that client change can be achieved from the session, but the client doesn't believe this, then the 'feel' of the work will be of the therapist pulling along a client who will resist the therapist's pace. If the client thinks that they can achieve what they want from the session and the therapist doesn't, then the 'feel' of the work will be of the client being frustrated at being held up by the therapist.
>
> (Dryden, 2019a: 87)

I go on to say that, '[e]ven if both therapist and client hold realistic expectations of what the latter can achieve from SST, if the therapist pushes for change, it may not happen' (Dryden, 2019a: 88). Thus, while expectations influence the outcome of SST, other therapeutic ingredients such as pacing and working together are also primary, as I will discuss in the second part of this book.

# Chapter 7

# SST Is a Fusion Between What the Client Brings to the Process and What the Therapist Brings to the Process

## Abstract

In this chapter, I argue that SST is a fusion of client and therapist factors, and, while the therapist helping the client to use extant strengths etc. is a key idea, there is nothing to stop the therapist offering the client something new so long as this is done in a way that empowers rather than disempowers the client.

## Introduction

As I argued in Chapter 5, SST is a mindset that the therapist brings to the work rather than a specific therapeutic approach. Thus, it is possible for therapists to practise SST in a variety of different ways but to be guided by the SST mindset in doing so. In this chapter, I will discuss the idea that SST is a fusion between what clients bring to the process and what therapists bring to the process.

## Client Empowerment

Hoyt et al. (2018b: 14–15) note that the concept of 'client empowerment' is a key feature of approaches to SST such as solution-focused, collaborative, narrative therapy and strengths-based therapy (which I call here the 'constructive' approaches). These approaches argue that what clients bring to the work is

DOI: 10.4324/9781003413103-8

the most significant contributory factor to the outcome of SST and that these factors include the following.

### Internal Strengths

Part of the therapist's SST mindset is the view that all clients have internal strengths that they have either overlooked or lost touch with, which potentially they can bring to the SST process and be helpful to them as they tackle their nominated issue.

### Values

When people are connected to their values, i.e., their judgments of what is important to them in their lives, this can have a profound effect on what they can achieve from SST. When a client sees that pursuing a goal is consistent with prized values, bearing this connection in mind is often highly motivating to the client.

### Previous Attempts to Solve the Problem

It is very likely that the client has attempted to solve their problem before coming to SST. To empower the client, the therapist will help them to identify and capitalise on those attempts that have had some positive impact in the past and that they can use in the future and to drop attempts that have not been helpful.

### Successful Attempts to Deal with Other Problems

When a client seeks therapy, it is likely that their focus will be on the problem that they have not solved. However, it is probable that they have solved other problems and it is empowering for them to focus on what they did to bring about change in these other areas and see that they can perhaps use these to solve the current problem.

### Helping Others

It is also likely that the client has had the experience of helping other people, perhaps even with the problem for which they are seeking help. Reminding the person of this and encouraging them to consider applying the helping factor(s) to their own current problem is part of the empowerment process.

### Being Helped by Others

It is also likely that the client has had the experience of being helped by others in the past either within therapy or outside. When the helping ingredients have been identified, this information may help the person apply them to themself, or it may help the therapist to help the client in a similar way.

### Role Models

A client may be inspired by people whom they admire. Having a client identify a role model relevant to the problem for which they are seeking help can accelerate the change process.

Sharoff (2002: 115–116) has outlined several steps that the SST therapist can use to help a client emulate a role model in the service of solving their problem:

1. *Help the client to identify the model.*
2. *Help the client to overcome resistance to being like the model.* The client may think a gap between themself and their chosen role model is too big. If so, you can either find ways to reduce the gap or help them choose a role model they can emulate.

3. *Help the client to see similarities between the role model and themself.* Unless the client sees such similarities, then the power of the role model as a facilitator of change is diminished.
4. *Be curious about the role model's outstanding skills and how they operate.* Doing so will encourage curiosity in your client about this issue.
5. *Help the client to identify the role model's skills and how they operate.* For a person to emulate a role model, they need to be clear about what they are emulating. Help the client gain such clarity.
6. *Agree with the client that they will implement these skills to address their nominated problem.*
7. *If necessary, educate the client about how to perform these skills.*

## Guiding Principles

My mother used to say to me, 'Son, if you don't ask, you won't get'. I often refer to this 'guiding principle' in my mind, if I am unsure about asking for something as a prelude to action. Helping the client to identify a relevant guiding principle can provide a significant impetus to change.

## External Resources

I distinguish between strengths that are internal to the person and resources that are external to the person. Such resources include people who can support the person during the change process and organisations that can provide help, information and support. The adage that states, 'only you can do it, but you do not have to do it alone' is particularly apt here (Lonergan, 2012). Helping the person to see that they can utilise such resources is significant when the contact between therapist and client is so short.

## Therapist Contributions

Therapists' contributions to SST are dependent on how they view the work. As I will discuss in Chapter 24, there are three major traditions in SST: constructive, active-directive and pluralistic. Perhaps the predominant tradition in SST is the constructive one, and thus I will emphasise it in this section. Hoyt et al. (2018b) argue that the major role of constructive therapists in SST is to help clients to identify and apply to the SST process the factors that I reviewed in the previous section. As they have eloquently put it, the role of the therapist in SST is to 'use their expertise primarily to help clients better use their own expertise' (Hoyt et al., 2018b: 15). They contrast constructive approaches with approaches 'in which change is primarily brought about by the therapist forming an opinion about what is wrong… and then proceeding to provide what the therapist discerns to be the needed remedy'. I will refer to these here as 'active-directive' approaches and will discuss them more fully in Chapter 24, in perhaps a more 'constructive' way (pun intended). There is a third growing tradition in SST that I call the pluralistic tradition. This tradition prioritises the client's viewpoint and advocates a both/and rather than an either/or approach to practice. Pluralistic practitioners are happy to utilise the strengths of the constructive and active-directive traditions without worrying too much about their different theoretical underpinnings.

### *Sharing Expertise versus Being the Expert*

I see SST as a fusion between what the client brings to the process and what the therapist brings to the process. The SST therapist should work to identify a whole host of client factors and encourage the clients to use them in the service of their goal. However, why should the therapist not *also* claim the freedom to ask the client if they are interested in hearing something that the client may not have thought of that may shed light on their problem and how to tackle it? Moreover, is it such a crime if this knowledge stems from the collective wisdom that underpins the therapist's own orientation? The therapist can show and use their expertise without coming across as 'the expert' in a way that disempowers the client. In short, in SST, it is possible for the therapist to *both* share expertise *and* empower the client.

## A Personal Example

In Appendix 1, I list 30 ideas that inform my practice of SST[1] – ten ideas that that are general in nature and 20 ideas that are informed by Rational Emotive Behaviour Therapy (REBT), a therapeutic approach that influences much of my work. In presenting this list, I want to make clear that, especially with respect to the REBT-informed ideas, I ask my clients if they are interested in my take on their issue and will ask this if they are struggling to make sense of their nominated problem themselves. If they have clarity on their problem and I can help them develop a solution from the variables outlined in the first half of this chapter, then there is no need for me to offer my insights.

These ideas are the ones that I have found particularly useful in informing my thinking and practice of SST. The beautiful thing about SST is that each SST therapist will have their own idiosyncratic list.

---

1 For a full discussion of these 30 ideas, see Dryden (2023b).

# Chapter 8

# SST Challenges Therapists' Cherished Beliefs about Therapy and Change

## Abstract

Whenever I give a presentation or workshop on SST, I warn the audience that what I have to say may challenge their valued ideas about therapy and psychological change. In doing so, I call upon them to listen to me with as much of an open mind as they can muster. Despite this, many therapists find themselves resisting SST. In this chapter, I consider and discuss some of the therapists' beliefs that SST challenges.

## A Therapist Needs to Develop a Good Therapeutic Relationships with a Client, and This Takes Time

It is clear from a number of reviews that the quality of therapeutic relationships is a vital variable in accounting for a good therapeutic outcome (e.g. Barkham & Lambert, 2021). While it may be the case that with specific clients it takes time to develop a sound working alliance, this is not universally so, and this latter notion challenges the beliefs of many therapists.

It is part of the SST mindset that therapists can develop a good working relationship with clients quickly and they do so by (i) taking seriously the client's presenting problem rather than considering that it hides the 'real' problem; (ii) negotiating with the client a realistic goal for the session that relates to the

DOI: 10.4324/9781003413103-9

presenting problem; (iii) getting down to work quickly and inviting the client to do the same; and (iv) showing that they are keen to provide help.

Simon, Imel, Ludman & Steinfeld's (2012) research showed that clients benefitting from SST report a strong working alliance with their therapists, while clients not benefitting from SST report a weak alliance with their therapists. Such research shows that it is entirely possible to form a good working relationship with clients quickly.

## More Is Better

The problem with the way therapists are trained is that such training most often centres on therapy that lasts much longer than the research indicates that many clients want. Thus, it is generally accepted that the modal number of sessions per treatment is 'one' internationally (Hoyt & Talmon, 2014b; Hoyt et al., 2018b). However, training courses rarely train students to offer SST and this, I believe, teaches them, albeit implicitly, that 'more is better'. However, research does not support this idea. Thus, Barkham & Lambert's (2021) review showed that the greatest amount of change occurs early in treatment rather than later and the amount of change clients experience diminishes as the number of sessions they have increases. My view is that if training courses train students to offer their clients SST and very brief forms of therapy, *as well as* longer-term therapy, the idea that 'more is better' would not be as prevalent as it currently is.

## Subjective Measures of Disturbance and Change Are Flawed, and Therefore It Is Best to Judge Change Objectively Rather than from the Client's Subjective View

Quite rightly, when psychotherapy is studied scientifically, it is important to use objective measures of change as well as subjective measures. However, in my view, there is too much reliance on the former as opposed to the latter when listening to clients report on what they received from SST. When clients seek help, it is because they are in subjective distress and not because of their score on an objective measure of disturbance. Just because SST clients may not have objectively made a 'clinically significant change' from a single session, the fact that they claim to have benefitted from it and are pleased with the service that they received should not be dismissed. Yes, subjective measures of disturbance are flawed, but so are human beings, so let's listen to what they have to say and, if they say that they have benefitted from SST, let's not dismiss it. After all, we did not dismiss it when they subjectively claimed to be disturbed when seeking help.

Also, there is nothing to say that SST therapists cannot use objective means to measure change as well as subjective measures. However, we would tend to privilege the latter as we would put the client and their views at the centre of the SST process.

### Psychologically Meaningful Change Happens Slowly and Gradually

As discussed above, professionals often distinguish between change that is clinically significant and change that is not. Clinically significant change occurs when someone moves outside the range of the dysfunctional population or within the range of the functional population (Jacobson, Follette & Revenstorf, 1984). Even when people acknowledge that therapeutic change does take place in SST, they dismiss it by saying that such change is not clinically significant. For clinically significant change, it is claimed, happens slowly and gradually. However, Hayes, Laurenceau, Feldman, Strauss & Cardaciotto (2007) have shown that, while clinically significant change can be gradual and linear, this is not universally the case and that such change can occur quite quickly. The possibility of a meaningful change occurring in a short period in SST challenges the commonly held idea that real change only occurs slowly and gradually.

Also, as noted above, who decides what is meaningful change and what isn't? Just because objectively the change a person makes in SST does not meet the criterion of clinical significance or meaningful change, it does not mean that subjectively it is not meaningful to the person.

## SST Is Not Suitable for Clients Facing Complex Problems

One of the most common questions asked by therapists first exposed to SST concerns the suitability of SST: 'Who is SST suitable for and for whom is it not suitable?' I discuss this issue in Chapter 10 (also see Dryden, 2022b).

Many SST therapists note that people with complex problems often seek simple solutions to these complex problems and are satisfied when they find such solutions within an SST framework (Hoyt et al., 2018b). Hoyt & Talmon (2014b: 503) reviewed several studies that show that 'the efficacy of SSTs is not restricted only to "easy" cases, but can have far-reaching effects in many areas, including treatment of alcohol and substance abuse as well as self-harming behavior'.

Chapter 9

# What Can and Cannot Be Achieved from SST

## Abstract

In this chapter, I consider what can and cannot be achieved from SST. I begin by making the obvious point that, in all probability, one session will not bring about quantum change. On the other hand, what a single session can do, among other things, is to help a person get unstuck, to change their behaviour and see its impact on another, to face and process adversity, and to leave a situation that is problematic for the person and where other forms of change are unlikely to happen.

## What Probably Cannot Be Achieved from SST

There is a concept in psychology known as quantum change, which shows that meaningful change can occur in a concise period both inside and outside psychotherapy. Quantum change refers to a sudden, dramatic and enduring change that affects a broad range of emotion, cognition and behaviour (Miller & C'de Baca, 2001). Perhaps the most well-known example of quantum change is Scrooge in Charles Dickens' short story, *A Christmas Carol*. Scrooge goes to bed on Christmas Eve, a curmudgeonly, miserly old man who hates Christmas, is generally nasty to everyone he knows and whose only love is money. During the night he is visited by three spirits, the ghosts of Christmas past,

DOI: 10.4324/9781003413103-10

Christmas present and Christmas yet to come. These spirits show Scrooge to himself in an increasingly negative light, culminating with his death mourned by nobody and whose grave is neglected. Scrooge promises to change to avoid this fate and does so. When he wakes up, he begins to treat everyone with kindness, generosity and compassion, embodying the spirit of Christmas. He literally changes overnight!

I have told this story to indicate what probably cannot be achieved with SST. Indeed, if a client sets this kind of change as an end-of-session goal the SST therapist, while not dismissing quantum change as an aspiration, would probably encourage the person instead to identify a sign that they had begun the journey towards this end.

## What Probably Can Be Achieved from SST

Having outlined what probably can't be changed in SST, let me now concentrate on what probably can be achieved. The following is a sample of what can realistically be achieved.

### Getting Unstuck

Quite often people come to therapy because they are stuck in a self-defeating pattern. Sometimes people unwittingly maintain their problems due to the fixed nature of their attempts to solve it. It is as if their car is stuck in snow and, the more they try to spin its wheels to free it from the snow, the more stuck the car gets. Helping a client to get unstuck is a viable goal in SST. While this can be done in several ways, perhaps the best way is to encourage the client to do something different (O'Hanlon, 1999).

*Doing something different.* Doing something different can help the client to break the vicious cycle that has developed where unsuccessful attempts to change lead to problem maintenance and to increased use of the unsuccessful change attempt. It is sometimes sufficient that, when the person takes one or two steps in a healthier direction, they sow the seeds for a virtuous cycle of change where new responses lead to more favourable responses from the environment.

### Changing Behaviour to Influence Others

People often come to therapy with the hidden (and sometimes not so hidden) agenda of changing someone with whom they have difficulty. While a change in another person is not within the control of the client, it may be in their sphere of influence. To this end, it may be useful to discuss with the client that the best way of bringing about a change in another is to bring about a change in oneself first. While this may mean a change in attitude, the only way the other person will be aware of this is by seeing it in the client's behaviour. So, as I often say to a client in SST: 'If you want to have a better relationship with the other, show them this by making a change in your behaviour so that they can see this'.

### Dealing with Adversity in More Constructive Ways

The foundation of my own SST practice is Rational Emotive Behaviour Therapy (Dryden, 2019b). My experience is that, when a person seeks therapy, it is because they experience difficulty in dealing with a recurring adversity (e.g. loss, failure, criticism). They may have tried to help themself deal with such adversities through avoidance and positive reframing, for example, but while such strategies afford people immediate relief, they do not help them face the adversity and process it in ways that help them going forward.

I have carried out many what I call 'very brief therapeutic conversations', which are one-off demonstration sessions of the way I work held in front of an audience (see Dryden, 2018a).

*Table 9.1* Common adversities and unhealthy negative emotions

| Adversity | Unhealthy Negative Emotions |
|---|---|
| • Threat | Anxiety |
| • Loss<br>• Failure<br>• Undeserved plight (self or other) | Depression |
| • Moral code violation (commission or omission)<br>• Hurting others | Guilt |
| • Acting in the past in a way I wish I had not done<br>• Failing to act in the past in a way I wished I had done | Unhealthy Regret |
| • Falling very short of my ideal<br>• Others negatively evaluate me | Shame |
| • Self is more invested in the relationship than the other is<br>• Important others treating me badly and I don't deserve such behaviour | Hurt |
| • Rule violation<br>• Threat to self-esteem<br>• Frustration<br>• Being treated with disrespect | Unhealthy Anger |
| • Other poses threat to an important relationship<br>• Uncertainty related to the above threat | Unhealthy Jealousy |
| • Other has something that I prize but do not have | Unhealthy Envy |

The person's emotions give a clue to the type of adversity that they are struggling with (see Table 9.1).

In my view, it is possible for the SST therapist to help the client deal with the adversity by facing it and processing it in ways that mean that they do not have to avoid it in the future or to put an unrealistic 'spin' on it. How they do this is going to be dependent on several factors, including their favoured therapeutic orientation and the client's experience of dealing with adversities, related to their problem or in general. I find that when I encourage an SST client to face and process the relevant adversity, they do emerge from this work with a different, more helpful perspective on the adversity and what it means to them and about them.

### Leaving Troublesome Circumstances

Sometimes a client comes to therapy with the goal of bringing about change in a troublesome set of circumstances or accepting these circumstances. An alternative that should be discussed with the client is to leave the circumstance when it is clear that the person has already made numerous attempts to change it and to accept it. This was the case with Martha, who was in an unsatisfying job with a boss who was 'allergic' to change, as she put it. She wanted some guidance about how she could bring him into the modern world or to accept her plight. I asked her why she was flogging a dead horse. Here is the relevant dialogue:

*Windy:*   Why not leave?
*Martha:*  Can I do that?
*Windy:*   What does your contract say?
*Martha:*  I have to give a month's period of notice.
*Windy:*   So, you have answered your own question.
*Martha:*  But what will happen to the company?

*Windy:*    It will go into liquidation, the second you leave.

*Martha:*    Very funny. I get your point.

*Windy:*    I haven't made a point.

*Martha:*    You are saying that I think I am the one keeping the company afloat.

*Windy:*    No, I'm not.

*Martha:*    That is stupid. I don't need to do that. I'm going to hand in my notice. Thanks.

*Windy:*    I haven't done anything.

I got an email from Martha five weeks later thanking me for giving her the courage to leave.

Chapter 10

# The 'Client Criteria' Question

## Abstract

In this chapter, I consider the oft-asked question concerning client indications and contra-indications. I present a variety of views on this question, including some client data, although we need to know more about this question from the client perspective.

## Introduction

When I give presentations and training courses in SST, the most frequently asked question concerns which clients benefit from SST and which do not (see Dryden, 2022b). While this question is reasonable, it is asked from the perspective of the therapist as if the therapist's opinion is the only one that matters. However, one of the guiding principles of SST is that the client's view should be prioritised. It seems from the literature that many clients tell us that they value the opportunity to come for one therapy session and not to return if they have got what they wanted (Hoyt & Talmon, 2014b). While that might be the end of the matter, in my view it is important to consider both the SST therapist's perspective and the client's when addressing what I call the 'client criteria' question.

DOI: 10.4324/9781003413103-11

## SST Therapists' Views on the 'Client Criteria' Question

SST therapists' views on the 'client criteria' can be summed up in the phrase, 'SST is not for clients who don't want it'. For all clients, if they want it they can have it, which is what open access is all about. If we consider this a little more closely, I will present the views of three groups of SST therapists: the 'SST-embedded' group, the 'SST open-access, enter now' group and the 'client choice' group.

### The 'SST-Embedded' Group

When SST is embedded in a service it is usually a service that offers other services and all sessions are by appointment. An example of the SST-embedded group is Jeff Young's approach (2018: 48–49), whose response to the question concerning who is suitable to SST and who is not is as follows:

> We believe the best response to this question is to avoid having to answer it by embedding SST in the service system so that clients can return if they want to. Embedding SST into the service system so that all services the organization normally provides are available following an initial session, conducted as if it may be the last, allows the practitioner and the organization to avoid the 'difficult if not impossible' decision of who is suitable and who is not suitable for a 'one-off' session. For many therapists and some managers, the assumption that clients facing complex problems require 'deep' change which can only occur in long-term work is powerful and entrenched. The SST literature continues to build data to challenge this assumption.

## The 'Open-Access, Enter Now' Group

The second group of SST therapists who do not advo-
cate a criteria-based approach to SST are those who work in
an open-access, enter now therapy service. By its nature,
open-access, enter now therapy offers therapy to whoever needs
it and uses the service. This is why it is also referred to as 'open
access'. If open-access, enter now clients are at risk, then the
purpose of the session is to help the client to be safe and access
other services if they want to. Open-access, enter now therapists agree with Young (2018) who says that it is rarely possible
to predict who will and will not benefit from SST in advance of
the session. Thus, in all forms of SST, the maxim is, 'The only
valid way to determine who may benefit from a single session of
therapy is to have the session with them and see if they benefit.'
If they do, they may have received the help they wanted or they
may request further help. If they don't, both client and therapist
will be clearer about the help that will benefit the client than if
they have a single assessment session.

## The 'Client Choice' Group

The third group of SST therapists who do not recommend
looking for and applying inclusion and exclusion criteria are
those that work in independent practice or in an agency where
client choice is paramount. Here, a client will discover or be
given information about the services offered by the therapist
or agency[1] and be encouraged to choose the service that best
offers the help they are looking for. It would be useful if current waiting times for each service can be made clear to the
client before they make their choice. If the client opts for SST,

[1] There will, of course, be therapy agencies who offer different therapy services but will want to decide for themselves which service to offer a client
based on assessment. This would be at variance with the core value in SST
that the client decides what is best for them, not the agency.

the practitioner will still want to assure themself that it is an informed choice before proceeding, given the importance of informed consent in this and other types of therapy delivery.

## Clients' Views on the 'Client Criteria' Question

In my book, *Very Brief Therapeutic Conversations* (Dryden, 2018a), I report on the problems that 245 people who volunteered for a brief 30-minute conversation tended to raise during that conversation (see Table 10.1). As can be seen from Table 10.1, 42 people were classified as presenting 'other emotional problems'. Table 10.2 provides a closer examination of the nature of such problems.

These tables show what one group of clients thinks it is appropriate to bring up in a SST setting. We need to find out more about what problems clients think they can bring to therapy that

*Table 10.1* Themes discussed in very brief therapeutic conversations (VBTCs) by category

| Theme Category | Total |
|---|---|
| Anxiety and Phobia | 49 |
| Problems with Procrastination | 39 |
| Anger Problems | 27 |
| Self-Esteem Problems | 27 |
| Problems with Uncertainty | 25 |
| Relationship Problems | 22 |
| Problems with Lack of Control | 14 |
| Other Emotional Problems | 42 |
| **Totals** | **245** |

Source: Dryden (2018a)

*Table 10.2* Themes raised by volunteers in the theme
category: other emotional problems

| | |
|---|---|
| Guilt | 13 |
| Hurt | 11 |
| Shame | 7 |
| Jealousy | 3 |
| Problem with Responsibility | 3 |
| Envy | 2 |
| OCD | 2 |
| Avoidance of Negative Feelings | 1 |
| **Other Emotional Problems: Total** | **42** |

Source: Dryden (2018a)

may last for a session (although further help is available) so that
we can get a fuller understanding of clients' perspectives on the
'client criteria' question.

# Chapter 11

# What Makes Good SST Therapists

## Abstract

If all clients do not benefit from SST, then all therapists are not suited to single-session work. In this chapter, I list and discuss several qualities that it is desirable for a therapist to have and/ or demonstrate for them to be a good SST therapist, in my view. The more of these qualities the therapist has and/or shows, the better they will be at delivering SST services.

## Having and Demonstrating an Enthusiasm for SST

While SST requires the therapist to develop and implement a good many skills, my view is that it is fundamental that the therapist is enthusiastic about single-session work. They need to have faith that they and their client can work together to help the client to get unstuck, for example, and move on with their life. They also need to enjoy the work and the challenge that SST affords. Personally, I find SST an energising way of working, which allows me to be creative. However, above all, the SST therapist needs to communicate their enthusiasm to the client while being mindful that there are other ways of working as well.

DOI: 10.4324/9781003413103-12

## Laying the Foundations for SST

Sometimes a client seeks out SST because they think they only need one session. This will be the case whether they seek SST by appointment or through an open-access, enter now service. Also, sometimes a client has not given much thought to the likely duration of therapy. They may never have heard of SST, so they will have had no reason to think it may be useful for them. In all such situations, the therapist needs to discuss with the client what SST offers and why the person may find it useful. This, of course, is with the usual proviso that further sessions are available if required. If the therapist lays the foundations for SST well, they get the session off to a good start so they can both get down to business and address the client's issue there and then.

## Expressing Themself with Clarity Throughout the Process

Since time is at a premium in SST (Dryden, 2016), the SST therapist can utilise the time they and their client have at their disposal by communicating clearly. It is better to err on the side of simplicity over complexity, but to do so without patronising the client. Without becoming obsessive about doing so, periodically, it is valuable to ask the client to put into their own words any substantive points that the therapist wants the client to grasp.

There may be key terms that the client and therapist use where it is crucial that they have a shared meaning of the term. Notably, where these terms are easily misunderstood, the therapist should make clear at the outset what they mean when they use the term. 'Acceptance' is one such term. I have learned that it saves time for me to clarify at the outset what I mean by the term if the client uses it or I want to use it. For example, if the client is anxious and wants to accept these feelings, I will ask them what they mean by the term, but I will also ask them if they would like to hear my take on acceptance. If they are interested, I say that first the client needs to acknowledge the existence of their anxious feelings. Second, they need to be clear with themself that they don't like feeling anxious and would prefer not to feel this way. Third, they recognise that they don't have to meet their preference in this respect.

## Creating and Maintaining an Agreed Therapeutic Focus

Most SST therapists will consider it a job well done if a client takes away one thing that will make a significant difference to their life. If this is to be achieved, the therapist will probably have to help the client create and maintain an agreed therapeutic focus. Such a focus incorporates the client's concern and realistic goal.

To do this, the good SST therapist checks with the client that they are both on the right track and that the therapist is able to interrupt the client with tact when the client begins to wander away from the agreed focus. See Chapter 23 for a more detailed discussion of this point.

## Maintaining the Client's Active Involvement During the SST Process

Anybody who has watched an excellent SST therapist at work will have seen a person who is able to be active themself while helping the client to maintain active involvement in the process as well. It is easy to fall prey to two errors as an SST therapist in this respect. The first error concerns the therapist failing to be sufficiently involved themself, which results in the client wandering from issue to issue without sufficient focus. The second error concerns the therapist being over-involved in the process, which results in the client adopting a complementary passive stance in the session. Guiding a middle course enables both therapist and client to work together in active harmony.

## Developing and Maintaining a Good Pace in the Session

While the SST therapist's contribution is vital in SST, most people would say that the client's contribution is central. However, a good outcome depends on them working together, but at a pace that will produce a good outcome. In this respect, I like to think that the therapist is like an accomplished pace-maker in a race that the client needs to win. The pacemaker ensures that the race is run at a pace that is neither too quick to prevent the client from burning out towards the end, nor too slow to prevent other runners from winning. However, it is also crucial that the pacemaker does not win the race. Instead, they need to bring the client along with them so that the client passes them before the end to win the race.

If the session is very speedy, the client will not process matters sufficiently and may end up confused, and, if it is too slow, time will have run out before anything meaningful has been achieved. A good pace facilitates client processing and increases the chances that a meaningful conclusion will be reached, and a good SST therapist has the skills and sense of timing to help the client in both respects.

## Looking For and Working Well with Clients' Strengths

Most therapists in the SST community consider that one of the key ingredients of a good outcome is the extent to which the therapist can help the client to identify and reconnect with their strengths[1] in a meaningful way so that the client can use these in the construction and execution of an agreed solution to their problem. A focus on just 'what is wrong' will not achieve this.

---

1  By strengths here, I mean all those client variables I discussed in Chapter 7.

A good SST therapist asks their client for their strengths directly and also looks for and identifies client strengths in their narrative. In both cases, the therapist will guide the client to use these strengths at critical moments in the SST process.

## Co-creating a Solution to the Client's Problem

When the client comes to therapy with a problem, the good SST therapist helps them set a session goal and, if necessary, a problem-related goal. They will help the client find a solution to the problem, enabling them to move towards the problem-related goal. In this respect, by 'solution', I mean something the client does to render the previous problem non-problematic and move them closer to the problem-related goal. Frequently, the solution gives concrete expression to the client's session goal (e.g. 'I want to find some ways of dealing with my anxiety').

The good SST therapist can work with the client to co-create a solution with the client that the latter can practise in the session and implement after the session. SST services that specialise in family work often utilise a team of observing therapists and participating therapist(s) (see chapters in Hoyt & Talmon, 2014b and Hoyt et al., 2018b). At an opportune moment towards the end of the session, the participating therapist(s) will take a break and consult with the therapy team, where specific solutions will be discussed so that one or more can be taken back into the room to be processed with the family. SST therapists who work by themselves sometimes do this too to give themselves thinking time. However, no matter which 'solution' is taken back into the room, it is good practice in SST that any solution that the client takes forward into their life is one to which they have actively signed up, if not co-created. The good SST therapist ensures that the latter happens whenever possible (see Chapter 27).

## Ending with Hope

I have argued earlier in this chapter that getting the single session off to a good start is a characteristic of the good SST therapist. So is bringing the session to a suitable end. A good ending in SST is one where there are no loose ends, the work done in the session has been adequately summarised by the client (preferably), the therapist or both, the client has a clear idea where to go next and the position on the possibility of future help has been made clear. The therapist who does all this and does it while engendering a sense of hope in the client that what has been done in the session can make a real difference to the person's life is a good SST therapist (see Chapter 29).

# Chapter 12

# For Better or for Worse

## Context Matters

### Abstract

In this chapter, I consider the importance of context on SST. First, I argue that SST is best practised within a setting that provides help at the point of need rather than help at the point of availability. Then, I consider other conducive organisational factors to the development of SST services.

## Introduction

In the previous chapter, I considered several qualities of good SST therapists. However, no matter how talented an SST therapist may be, if that person works in a context that is not conducive to the practice of effective SST, then such talent is likely to be wasted. On the other hand, if the context in which the therapist works is conducive to the practice of SST, this context enables the therapist to encourage the client to get the most out of the session.

## Conducive Pathways

In Chapter 4, I argued that SST is best practised when it is embedded in a service that offers clients help at the point of need rather than help at the point of availability, and I refer the reader to that chapter for a detailed discussion of this issue. Suffice it to say, SST thrives in agencies where help is offered

DOI: 10.4324/9781003413103-13

at the point of need (such as open-access, enter now clinics) and struggles in agencies where help is provided only at the point of availability. Thus, it is not a good idea for an agency to set up an SST service where clients for SST would have to go on a long waiting list. If a service is thinking of offering SST, its key personnel need to consider what changes the agency needs to make to offer clients help at the point of need.

Young (2018) presents research that details the fact that, in a three-year period in community counselling centres in Victoria, Australia, 42% of clients attended for one session, 18% for two sessions and 10% for three sessions. The greater the number of sessions, the fewer the number of clients who attended them. This shows that, while an agency may be organised to allow for the possibility that clients may only attend once, that agency needs to offer other services as well. As Young (2018) says, he wants to offer excellent service both to the 42% of clients that attend only once and to the 58% who attend more than once.

## Embedded SST

Unless an organisation only offers SST (e.g. an open-access, enter now service which does nothing else apart from offering this kind of help), then SST needs to be integrated with an agency's other services. In doing so, it will be and will be seen to be an integral part of the total services on offer. When this happens, the SST service will make and receive referrals from other services, and over time it will become embedded into the agency's overall provision. To facilitate this, all interested therapists should contribute to SST, and SST therapists should contribute to the other services.

Another model in which SST is embedded within an agency's provision is where everyone is seen for a single therapy session rather than an assessment (which is the norm in agencies). At the end of the session, or after an agreed period of time, the client decides whether or not to seek more help. As Young notes, knowing that further help is possible allows clients to be 'held' and rely on their resources more (see also Chapter 10).

## Service Care

Young (2018) has made the point that it is one thing for SST thinking and services to be introduced into an agency and sit alongside, shape and be shaped by existing services, it is another thing for SST to thrive in this context. As Young (2018: 41) notes:

> if an organization does not keep SST alive with ongoing activities such as evaluation, research, and/or reflective supervisory practices, and if it is not embedded in policy, core practice and key processes, SST-inspired service delivery is lucky to survive beyond five years... This is especially likely if key supporters of the approach leave the organization.

In other words, the agency in which SST therapists work needs to care for the professional well-being of its staff so that therapists can maintain enthusiasm for working in an SST-inspired environment to help them maintain their creativity in the application of SST (see Dryden, 2023, for a fuller discussion of this issue).

# Chapter 13

# The Importance of the Working Alliance

## Abstract

In this chapter, I use the updated four-component working alliance framework to shed light on the SST process. I argue that, when the client and therapist have a robust and collaborative bond, share similar views of facets of this process, negotiate realistic client goals and work together to find a solution that facilitates goal attainment, there will tend to be a good outcome from the meeting.

## Introduction

In my opinion, one of the most useful ideas in psychotherapy is Bordin's (1979) concept of the working alliance. According to Bordin (1979), the working alliance is comprised of three components: bonds, goals and tasks. Later, I added a fourth component, views (Dryden, 2006, 2011). In this chapter, I will use the updated working alliance framework to show how SST therapists can help clients get the most out of the first and perhaps only session that they may have.

## Bonds

Bonds refer to the interconnectedness between therapist and client. There are several ways of understanding this interconnectedness. I will discuss two such ways: the role of the 'core

DOI: 10.4324/9781003413103-14

conditions' in SST and the importance of developing a collaborative relationship.

## Core Conditions

Rogers (1957), in a seminal article, spelt out a number of conditions that clients need to experience from their therapists if they are to gain from therapy. These 'core conditions', as they are popularly known, have undergone revision over the years, but are widely known as empathy, respect and genuineness.

*Empathy.* Time is of the essence in SST. Given this, while the SST therapist needs to create space for the client to express themself, this space usually needs to be limited to one issue that, if resolved, will make a difference to the client's life. Within this space, it is vital for the client to experience the therapist's understanding of their struggles with the problematic issue. What I call 'empathy with a twist' is the therapist conveying an understanding of the client's struggles plus communicating a sense of hope that things could be different.

*Respect.* When a therapist shows a client respect in SST, they communicate that the client is a fallible human being with strengths and weaknesses and they can use the former to help with their problem/issue. Also, the SST therapist shows respect to the client by placing the client's choice, self-determination and empowerment centre stage in the change process.

At a more practical level, SST therapists sometimes need to interrupt clients to help them keep on track. Many therapists find doing so tricky given their prior training not to interrupt their clients' flow. One way of interrupting a client that shows respect for that client is to give a rationale for interrupting them and asking permission to do so.

*Genuineness.* Being honest and giving authentic responses to a client indicate the therapist's wish to have a real relationship with the client in SST. Nowhere is this more prevalent than in Young's 'No Bullshit Therapy' – NBT (see Findlay, 2007). Here is what Young (2018: 55) says about his approach:

NBT is enacted by creating a context where a therapist (and client) can be honest and direct, where the therapist can challenge from a good and caring place, can marry honesty and directness with warmth and care, and promote transparency and reduce obfuscation by avoiding jargon... Creating transparency in keeping with the philosophy of SST with mandated clients may look like stating how you prefer to work and seeking the client's response ('I like to be pretty upfront and direct; how does that fit with you?'), rather [than] making the assumption that the client wants to collaborate with you.

Transparency is an important part of SST. When an SST therapist is being transparent, they are being genuine and clear about such matters as (i) what SST is and it isn't; (ii) what they can and cannot do as an SST therapist, and (iii) what services are available to the client if they wish to access more help together, with a likely waiting time for each service.

### Collaboration

While mandated clients probably won't collaborate in SST, most clients have chosen to seek therapy and will collaborate with their therapist. The collaborative bond involves the following features:

- SST is client-directed, but with the therapist sharing any concerns about the direction with the client.
- The therapist and client are explicit about what is the client's nominated issue/problem and what are the latter's session and problem-related goals (see Chapter 22).
- The therapist and client negotiate the therapeutic focus (see Chapter 23).
- The therapist and client work together to find a solution (see Chapter 27).

- SST is a fusion between what the client brings to the process and what the therapist brings to the process (see Chapter 7).
- The therapist and client negotiate about further help for the client if the client thinks they need it and agree on a pathway for the client to use, if necessary (see Chapter 29).
- The therapist and client negotiate about follow-up – if it is to occur and when (see Chapter 30).

## Views

The 'views' component of the working alliance concerns the ideas that both participants hold about salient ideas of the SST process. The important point about these ideas is that the therapist and client end up by agreeing on their respective views even if they may hold different ideas at the outset.

In my opinion, there are three main areas where client and therapist need to have such agreement.

### Views on the Service

It is vital that the client and therapist agree on what SST means for them in the particular situation that they are in. Does it mean only one session, and that is it, or can the client have further sessions if they want to? If they request and are offered further help, can these sessions be booked one at a time (as in OAATT) or can the client book a series of sessions?

### Views on the Problem and What Accounts for It

If a SST therapist works with a client's problem as well as helping them to find a solution, rather than just being solution focused, it is vital that they have an agreed understanding of the client's problem and what accounts for it. This is the case whether the therapist shares their professional understanding of the client's problem or whether the therapist elicits the client's view on the same problem. If they do not share a negotiated view of the problem, they may work at cross-purposes.

### *Views on Therapy for the Problem*

It is also vital that the client and therapist have a joint understanding about how this problem can best be tackled. If not, they will again work at cross-purposes, and the session will not be fully utilised. When solutions are discussed, it is crucial that the solution is negotiated and that both can see that it has the potency to help the client to achieve their problem-related goal, if implemented.

In family-oriented SST, the sessions are often watched by an observing team whose primary purpose is to arrive at a solution that the family is likely to implement to help them achieve their goals. The observing team suggests this to the therapist (or therapist team) when they take a break from the session. If such a solution is to 'work', all three parties need to agree that this proposed solution has sufficient therapeutic potency in this respect.

## Goals

All therapy is purposive, and this is especially the case with SST. What is specific to SST with respect to goals is that the client is asked to specify a goal for the end of the session (e.g. 'If at the end of the session you thought that you got what you were hoping for, what would that be?') rather than a goal for the end of treatment. However, the SST therapist might also negotiate a goal with the client regarding the problem they want to discuss (which I call the nominated problem). I refer to this as the problem-related goal. The following diagram details the relationship between the two sets of goals.

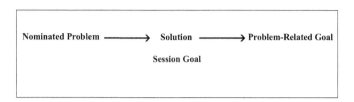

What this diagram shows is that frequently what the client wants from the session (i.e. their session goal) is to find a solution to their nominated problem. The client's task is to implement the solution (session goal), which will help them to achieve their problem-related goal.

In SST, it is probably better to negotiate specific goals than general ones. However, if the latter is agreed, it is paramount that both client and therapist are clear about how they will both know if these goals are achieved. However, it is useful to recognise that, in SST, the therapist will usually not know if the client has achieved their goal unless a follow-up session is carried out (see Chapter 30).

The critical point about goals from a working alliance perspective is that the client and therapist agree on the client's goals so that they can work together to achieve them. If not, the single session has the quality of the client resisting the efforts of the therapist to take them in a direction to which they have not agreed, however 'healthy' such a goal may be.

## Tasks

Tasks are activities carried out by both client and therapist that are in the service of the client's goals. Again, from a working alliance perspective, it is vital for the client and therapist to have an understanding of one another's tasks, either explicitly or implicitly, and agree that the execution of these tasks is a useful way forward.

In Chapter 11, I argued that a solution is a response to a problem that helps the client to achieve their problem-related goal. As I pointed out earlier in this chapter, it is crucial for the therapist and client to agree on the nature of the solution. Here, it is vital for the client to see that they can execute the solution and that doing so will help them achieve their goal.

As I will discuss in Chapter 28, it can be valuable for the client to practise the chosen solution with the therapist in the session before using it in outside life. When this is done, the more the client believes that they can carry out the task and that it will be useful for them to do so, the more likely it is that they will do it.

After therapy ends, the client is left to implement the solution themself without direct therapeutic help. The client can be prepared to do this if the therapist can guide them through this process using imagery to do so.

## Conclusion

The working alliance framework is a useful way of thinking about the practice of SST from a general point of view that can be used by therapists from different orientations. A good working relationship between therapist and client in SST can be formed very quickly and, when it does, it yields a good outcome (Simon et al., 2012). This framework can help explain why.

# Chapter 14

# From Theory to Practice I

## Guidelines for Good Practice

### Abstract

In this chapter, I consider four main theoretical SST principles and discuss how they lead to guidelines for good SST practice. The principles are:

- One session may be enough. Help the client get the most out of it, whether or not another one is needed.
- The session is important, but not all important.
- It is best to go slowly, be steady and be humble.
- Show genuine optimism about what clients are capable of.

Many writers on SST have developed lists of the do's and don'ts of good practice in SST (e.g. Bloom, 1992; Paul & van Ommeren, 2013 and Talmon, 1990). In this chapter, I consider guidelines for good practice but link them to the key theoretical principles as summarised above.

## One Session May Be Enough. Help the Client Get the Most Out of It, Whether or Not Another One Is Needed

One of the key theoretical assumptions of SST is what may be called 'the flexible power of the one'. By which is meant

DOI: 10.4324/9781003413103-15

there is a lot that can be achieved if client and therapist 'roll up their sleeves' and deal with the client's nominated issue, and this power can be harnessed if the therapist follows SST mindset-inspired guidelines. However, all the work does not have to be done in this one session; further sessions are possible.

This assumption spawns the following guidelines for good practice, which will help the client get the most from the session, whether or not it is the only one they have.

### Engage the Client Quickly Through the Work

The therapist utilising all their time with the client is a central part of SST. Thus, the therapist gets down to work as quickly as possible. As discussed in the previous chapter, the bond between therapist and client is strengthened when this happens. Also, the client gets the sense that the therapist is keen to help, which results in the client joining the therapist in this endeavour.

### Be Clear about Why You Are Here

Therapist clarity aids the SST process in the sense that both the therapist and client know why they are there and what their common task is. In this way, any client misconceptions about the purpose of the session can be identified, discussed and resolved.

### Be Prudently Active

The therapist needs to take an active role but one that also encourages the client to be active. Active collaboration is a feature of effective SST.

## Be Focused and Help the Client Stay Focused

When the therapist helps the client to create a focus for the session, this should ideally be based on the client's view of their problem and what they want to achieve in relation to that problem.[1] Once the focus has been created, the therapist helps the client stay focused.

## Develop a Negotiated Solution

In one sense, all SST is solution-focused in that the therapist strives with the client to find a solution that will deal with the client's nominated problem and help with goal attainment. Tentative solutions may be put forward by both and then discussed, culminating in the client selecting the one that has the most meaning for them and is most likely to work.

## Practise the Solution in the Session

Once a solution has been selected, the client can practise this in the session, if feasible. This immediate practice helps the client see what it feels like to implement the solution and what modifications may be necessary.

## Help the Client to Develop an Action Plan

Once the client has committed themself to the solution, it is important that the therapist helps them to develop a plan of action that will encourage them to implement this solution in their everyday life.

---

1  This may not apply to solution-focused single-session therapists who tend to eschew working with problems.

### *Tie Up Loose Ends and Discuss Possible Future Sessions*

It is essential that the session is ended on a high note, if possible, with the therapist answering any client questions and responding to any client doubts, reservations and objections. Part of a good closure concerns the situation regarding further sessions. The client needs to know what to do if they need further help in the near future or further down the line.

### The Session Is Important, But Not All Important

One of the ironies of SST (and there are many) is that, while there is much potential power to harness from the first (and perhaps only) session, the session is not all important in the change process. There is also much the client can gain from all that life has to offer, and encouraging clients to develop such a mindset means that they will continue a process of change that started even before they had the session.

### *Help the Client to See That Change May Have Already Started*

It often happens that, when a person has decided to seek help, they initiate a process of change that sometimes results in them cancelling any session they may have booked with a therapist. If the client does attend therapy, the SST therapist enquires to see what has changed since they decided to seek help and encourages the client to capitalise on any changes that they have made.

### *External Resources May Be as Helpful as Internal Strengths*

The SST therapist knows that there is a wealth of external resources in the client's environment they can draw upon to help solve their problem. Orienting the client to this can be liberating for the client, who realises that only they can do it, but they do not have to do it alone.

### Extra-Therapy Events Can Help the Client to Change

Several years ago, a man booked a single session with me and, the night before the session, he went out for a meal with some friends. At that meal, he opened up to them about his problem and got a tremendously supportive response from them with several saying they, too, had also struggled with what he was struggling with. He found the evening profoundly therapeutic and only came to see me out of courtesy. I reinforced some of what he had concluded from the night before, and he left. I had done very little. He did the real work the night before with his friends.

SST therapists are happy to hear such stories because we know that change can come from a myriad of sources and not just from a single session.

## It Is Best to Go Slowly, Be Steady and Be Humble

You might think it strange that slowness, steadiness and humility underpin SST practice. Surely it should be: quickness, animation and supreme confidence?

### Take Your Time

When a single-session therapist knows what they are doing, they know that the best way to conduct the session is slowly. Working at a fast speed is often fuelled by anxiety, and an anxious SST therapist will not do an adequate job. It is surprising how much ground can be covered when an SST therapist works slowly and carefully, but in a focused manner with a client.

### One Step Forward May Be Enough to Get Change Under Way

Given SST's view of the change process as being something that probably started before the session and can continue after it, the SST therapist is happy if they have helped a client to take the first step because they know that, if they encourage the client to use their strengths and capabilities, then they have helped them to take a step in the right direction. The client can then take another step and another step etc., going forward.

### Be Honest When You Do Not Know

Many therapists are frightened to say 'I do not know' to clients for fear of looking bad in the client's eyes. However, the SST therapist knows the value of humility and that most clients actually appreciate such honesty. Furthermore, the therapist's view is that their skills are more important than knowledge in facilitating change in SST and, if they don't know something, they could always find out.

### Show Genuine Optimism about What Clients Are Capable Of

Without a genuinely optimistic outlook of what clients can achieve from SST, therapists will think that facilitating client change in SST is down to them. This results in them putting themselves under pressure, and SST therapists do not work well under pressure. Such optimism also has to be communicated to clients. There are a number of ways to do this as follows.

### Identify the Client's Strengths and Encourage Them to Use Them

A defining feature of SST is the emphasis on client empowerment and strengths. Helping clients to identify and reconnect with their strengths and then be asked to think about how they might apply these strengths to their current concern is a common strategy in SST. In doing so, the therapist shows the client that they have faith in the latter's capabilities, which helps them feel empowered.

### Identify Helpful Attempts to Solve the Current and Other Problems and Encourage Their Use

It is likely that the client has tried various things in the past to address their nominated problem, some of which may have yielded some benefit. If so, the therapist can help them to distil the helpful ingredients and encourage them to apply these anew to the problem, perhaps with some embellishments suggested by the therapist.

Also, the therapist can encourage the client to draw on what they did to solve other problems and use these helpful strategies to address their current concern. This can be seen as encouraging the client to get the most out of themself and, in doing so, to get the most out of the SST process.

### Encourage the Client to Take Away Learning from the Session and Apply It

In SST, the client is seen as capable of applying the negotiated solution to where it matters in their everyday life. However, they do need some encouragement to do so. In this regard, the therapist can suggest using action planning and mental rehearsal as useful ways of bridging the gap between practising the solution in the session and implementing it in the client's life.

Chapter 15

# From Theory to Practice II
## What to Avoid

### Abstract

I would say that the efficient use of time is one of the key principles of single-session therapy. Here, the therapist is mindful
that they may only have one session with the client, and as such,
they need to use this knowledge to intervene accordingly. In the
previous chapter, I outlined the types of interventions the SST
therapist makes when they are using time efficiently. In my view,
learning is enhanced when good practice is contrasted with bad
practice so, in this chapter, I do two things. First, I review activities that therapists may implement when they do not have the
efficient use of time at the forefront of their minds. This may be
the case with therapists who work within generous time limits
(e.g. 12–20 sessions) or who work with clients in an ongoing
manner where the end of therapy is not specified. Please note
that, in listing these activities, I am advising therapists to refrain
from their use not in absolute sense but when they are delivering
SST. Second, I review activities that stem from therapists being
intimidated by the time limits inherent in SST.

## When Time Is Not at a Premium

When therapists work conventionally with clients, they tend
to engage in a number of activities that I will review below.
These activities have merit given the context of the time such

DOI: 10.4324/9781003413103-16

therapists have with their clients. However, as we will see, they are not indicated when therapists deliver SST. In discussing each activity, I will give reasons why they are not recommended in SST.

### Taking an Elaborate History

Taking an elaborate history is vital in conventional therapy because it helps the therapist to understand the person within the rich context of their developing history. Each person is unique and is best understood when the following information is obtained:

- The client's upbringing and relationships with parents, siblings and other family members.
- The client's schooling and educational and social development (e.g. relationships with peers).
- The client's relationship and sexual history particularly with an emphasis on problematic aspects.
- The client's occupational history and relationships with bosses and work colleagues.
- The client's hobbies and recreational activities.
- The client's history of psychological problems and especially any episodes of suicide attempts and self-harm.
- The client's problematic use of substances (e.g. alcohol and drugs).
- The client's history of physical problems.
- Current evidence of risk of harm to self and others.

In taking a history, the therapist is looking for patterns that may relate to current problems.

*SST view: Don't take an elaborate history.* In the film *Ghost Town*, Ricky Gervais plays a cynical New York dentist who goes to A&E complaining of bowel problems. At intake, he is asked some questions about his history to which he replies 'irrelevant'. This is a good reminder for the SST therapist only to ask questions that are relevant to the client's concerns. The therapist does not have the time or the reason to take an elaborate history.

My own take on this issue is that I will ask my SST clients a question such as, 'Is there anything you think I need to know about your history that, if I didn't know, you think I would not be able to help you today?' This puts the responsibility on the client to tell me crucial aspects of their history in a contained way.

### Letting the Client Talk in an Unfocused Way

When clients come to therapy, they may experience for the first time an opportunity to talk about themselves in whichever way they choose, free from the constraints of other people's agendas. The therapist only has one agenda: to listen to the client and provide them with help in an unrushed environment. Additionally, coming to therapy may be the first time the client has had an opportunity to talk about themselves in a personal way. For both of these reasons, it is vital for the client to talk in their own way, at their own pace.

*SST view: Don't let the client talk in an unfocused, general way.* In general, left to their own devices, clients will talk about their concerns in a general way without focus, as noted above. Given that time is at a premium in SST, such general, unfocused talk will not help the client to get much out of the single session. Working with specificity and focus is what is needed in SST.

### Listening and Responding from the Client's Frame of Reference

As we have seen, it is important to give new clients an extended opportunity to talk in their own way at the beginning of therapy. The therapist's role here is to listen attentively and non-judgmentally and not impose a direction on the client. While the client is exploring themself in this unfocused way, the therapist seeks to convey their understanding of the client from their frame of reference. The therapist does not impose time limits on themself concerning how long they will stay in this mode of listening and responding, as they take the client's lead. When the client becomes more focused so will the therapist.

*SST view: Don't spend too much time in non-directive, listening mode.* While it is important for the client in SST to be heard, the SST therapist ensures they give their non-judgmental attention to the client while helping them to focus on their prime concern. They consequently do not spend too much time in a non-directive, listening mode.

### Assessing Problems Comprehensively

In therapy free from time pressure, the therapist has the time to do a thorough assessment of the problems that clients present for help. As it is not clear what may be relevant and what may not be relevant, the therapist errs on the side of caution and collects a lot of data even though they may not use much of this information later. From this perspective, it is better to have something and not use it than miss something that was crucial.

*SST view: Don't assess where not relevant.* Not all SST therapists engage in problem assessment, but those who do avoid assessing areas that may be useful to know about but is unnecessary to the focus of SST. In my practice of SST, I usually spend much time in problem assessment mode. In particular, it is vital for me to know precisely what adversities my clients struggle with and how they inadvertently maintain their problem. However, this assessment is done in a focused way, with little, if any, unnecessary data gathering (Dryden, 2018a, 2022a).

### Carrying out a Case Conceptualisation

Case conceptualisation involves the therapist and client working together to gain an overall picture of the factors that account for the development and maintenance of the client's problems and how they may be linked. Increasingly, in CBT, the view is that it is best not to initiate treatment unless one has carried out such a conceptualisation as this would be like trying to get somewhere unfamiliar without a map. It may take two or three sessions to develop such a conceptualisation. Also, if an elaborate history has been taken, then we may be into the fifth or sixth session before intervention starts. This is not an issue in longer-term therapy as long as the client understands and agrees with the rationale for these activities.

*SST view: Don't carry out an elaborate case conceptualisation.* While carrying out a case conceptualisation may be a valuable exercise, there is no time in SST for the therapy dyad to engage in it and this is why I say that SST is assessment, not conceptualisation driven (Dryden, 2022a). This poses a challenge for those CBT therapists who find it difficult to intervene without being guided by a case conceptualisation.

My view is that I agree that SST therapists do not have the time to carry out a full case conceptualisation. However, I think that they can be informed by case conceptualisation ideas, particularly when doing a focused assessment of the client's nominated problem.

### When the SST Therapist Is Intimidated by Time

Some therapists are intimidated by the idea that they may have only one session to help the person. My hunch is that such a therapist holds the attitude that they must use time effectively and that they must help the person within this timeframe and that they cannot tolerate the limits inherent in SST. If this is the case, I recommend that the therapist develop a flexible attitude towards time and helping and learn to tolerate the limits, which will help them to see the advantages that there are in working within such limits (see Chapter 3 and the case of Rod Temperton).

When a therapist is intimidated by time they tend to:

### Rush and Overload Their Client

The time-intimidated SST therapist has an idea of what they want to cover in a session and rushes through it rather than focusing on one or two key points. They struggle with the SST view that 'less is more'. The result is that the client feels rushed, uncomfortable and confused.

*SST antidote: Don't rush the client.* Just because time is at a premium in SST (Dryden, 2016), it does not follow that SST therapists rush their clients. In fact, those who do are generally ineffective. I often point to the example of Mesut Özil, the ex-Arsenal footballer, who was very effective, but never seemed to be in a rush. Good SST therapists take their time!

### Assume That Their Client Knows What They (the Therapist) Are Doing and Why

Here, the therapist thinks that they do not have the time to explain their interventions and the reasons for making them even if they pick up that their client may have doubts about what they are doing. Actually, given that the therapist is under time pressure, they probably won't even pick up that the client may have such doubts.

*SST antidote: Don't assume that the client knows what the therapist is doing or why they are doing it.* It is tempting for therapists to think that, if clients give non-verbal signs that they understand what their therapists are doing and the reasons for doing it, then they do, in fact, understand. Good SST therapists do not make this assumption and will err on the side of caution by explaining what they do and why they are doing it. Moreover, they think that they have the time to do it.

### Ask Multiple Questions

If the client pauses to think about their answer to a question, the time-intimidated SST therapist considers this as time wasted and asks another version of the question or a different question entirely.

*SST antidote: Don't ask multiple questions.* SST therapists tend to ask many questions but show patience in doing so. They avoid asking clients multiple questions if answers are not quickly forthcoming. Good SST therapists give their clients time to think.

We have now reached the end of the theoretical part of the book. In Part 2, I will discuss the distinctive features of the practice of SST.

# Practice

# Chapter 16

# Overview

## The Process of SST

### Abstract

In this chapter, I consider two perspectives on the process of SST. These will serve as an overview for the rest of the chapters in the practical part of this book. The first perspective is perhaps more relevant to where the therapist is working alone. Following Hoyt (2000), there are six phases of SST: (i) decision; (ii) preparation; (iii) beginning; (iv) middle; (v) ending; and (vi) follow-through and follow-up. I briefly discuss what tends to happen at each phase. The second perspective is perhaps more relevant to open-access, enter now therapy and where there is a team approach. Following McElheran, Stewart, Soenen, Newman & MacLaurin (2014), there are five phases of SST: (i) pre-session; (ii) the session with a focus on the presenting issue; (iii) an inter-session consultation; (iv) delivery of the intervention; and v) post-session debriefing.

## Perspective 1: Where the Therapist Is Working Alone

It is not unusual for therapists to take a process view of therapy (e.g. Garfield, 1995) and this perspective is most likely to be taken when therapy lasts for longer than a single session. However, Hoyt (2000) has brought a process perspective to SST, and I have drawn on his ideas in this chapter.

DOI: 10.4324/9781003413103-18

### The Decision Phase

In the decision phase, the person seeking help has contacted the therapist, and the two of them need to decide whether or not they both want to engage in SST and whether or not this way of working best meets the person's therapeutic needs. I discuss this issue in greater detail in the next chapter.

### The Preparation Phase

Hoyt et al. (2018b) distinguish between SST by appointment and SST by open-access, enter now. In the former, the therapist gives the client an opportunity to prepare for the session so that they can get the most out of the process. This preparation is most often done by the client completing and returning a pre-session questionnaire (see Chapter 19).

### The Beginning Phase

After contracting (see Chapter 18), the beginning phase of SST is marked by the therapist enquiring of the client what problem they want to address and/or what goal they want to achieve from the session (see Chapter 22). If they mention a longer-term goal, the therapist still helps them to set a session goal, which is framed as a step towards the longer-term goal. By getting down to work straight away and demonstrating a keenness to help the client, the therapist establishes a good working alliance with the client (see Chapter 13).

### The Middle Phase

Once the therapist and client know what the client wants to achieve, they get down to the business of what Hoyt calls 'refocus and change'. This is the phase where SST therapists bring to the process the insights and skills offered by their own therapeutic orientations and use them within the context of empowering the client by drawing on and encouraging them to use their inner strengths, competencies, resiliency factors and helping them to see how they can utilise their external resources (see Chapter 25). This is what I have called the SST fusion between what the client brings to the process and what the therapist brings to the process (see Chapter 7). Thus, in the middle phase, the therapist may work with the client to consider implementing a variety of potential solutions (see Chapters 24 and 27). These include (i) identifying exceptions to their problem occurring and helping the client capitalise on these; (ii) looking for and utilising instances of the goal happening; (iii) encouraging the client to do something different; and (iv) looking at things from a different perspective. The creative SST therapist often invents tailor-made interventions on the spot that are impactful and encourage the client to develop creative solutions that address their problems and/or facilitate movement towards their goal (see Chapter 26).

Later in the middle phase, the therapist helps the client to select a solution that they think will be most helpful to them (see Chapter 27), and encourages them, if possible, to practise the solution in the session (see Chapter 28) and to make plans to implement this learning.

### The Ending Phase

In the ending phase, the therapist encourages the client to summarise what they have learned from the session and to see how they can generalise their takeaways. The therapist answers any last-minute questions that the client may have and generally ties up loose ends (see Chapter 29). An agreement is made concerning whether future sessions are possible and, if they are, what the client has to do to access these.

## The Follow-Through and Follow-Up Phase

From one perspective this is not a part of the SST process since the person may not return. From another perspective, it is a part of the SST process, especially when it is framed as OAATT, where the client can have a series of single sessions, if desired. Hoyt (2000) makes the useful distinction between follow-through, which concerns matters of client continuation and return, and follow-up, which concerns gaining feedback from the client concerning outcome and service evaluation after therapy has finished (see Chapter 30).

## Perspective 2: Open-Access, Enter Now Therapy and Where Therapists Work in a Team

In describing open-access, enter now therapy at Eastside Family Centre in Calgary, Alberta, Canada, McElheran, Stewart, Soenen, Newman & MacLaurin (2014) describe a different process of an SST session. This process view differs from the one described above in that it describes an approach to open-access, enter now therapy where the client is a family rather than an individual who are helped by a therapy team as opposed to a therapist working alone. This process perspective is consistent with the Milan family therapy model (e.g. Boscolo, Cecchin, Hoffman & Penn, 1987) and appears to describe a lot of SST work with families carried out by therapists who are supported by an observing team.[1]

## The Pre-Session

This involves a review of any forms filled out by the client and of any other information to hand (e.g. notes if there has been

---

1 I will refer here to 'client' and 'therapist' even though the client may be a family and there may be more than one person in the role of therapist.

previous contact by the client). The team formulate tentative hypotheses as a possible guide for the session and for testing within the session.

## The First Half of the Session

Here the client discusses why they are seeking help, and the therapist helps them to focus and address the presenting issue.

## The Inter-Session Consultation

The treating therapist calls for a break and consults with the therapy team about the issue that has been co-created by the client and therapist, and the whole team discusses and puts forward an intervention. In some agencies, this discussion is done with the family members present, who actively participate in the construction of the intervention.

## The Second Half of the Session

The therapist offers commendations to the client and delivers the intervention on behalf of the therapy team.

## The Post-Session Debriefing

After the client leaves, the therapy team discuss whether or not the client got what they wanted from the session, and a note is made to guide future work if the client returns.

While two different perspectives on the process of SST have been presented, I will mainly use the first one to structure the rest of the book, although many issues discussed will be relevant to both perspectives.

Chapter 17

# Making a Decision about SST

## Abstract

In this chapter, I consider the issue of helping a person decide whether or not SST will be helpful to them. In doing so, I use a help-seeking framework that outlines the roles that a person may occupy when contacting a therapist or therapy service.

## Introduction

When a person approaches a therapist or a therapy service, they occupy one of three help-seeking roles. It is useful for the SST therapist and the person who takes such calls in a therapy agency to consider which role a person may occupy when deciding whether or not a person may benefit from SST. This tends only to apply to SST by appointment rather than SST by open-access, enter now, where the therapist needs to deal with the person no matter which of the following roles they may occupy.

## Different Help-Seeking Roles

There are a number of roles that a person may occupy with respect to help-seeking (see Seabury, Seabury & Garvin, 2011). I will consider this issue concerning my practice.

DOI: 10.4324/9781003413103-19

### The 'Explorer' Role

When a person is in the 'explorer' role, they recognise that they have a problem and are thinking about what to do about it. If they have decided to think about seeking help, they have not made any direct approaches to potential helpers. Instead, they may have spoken to people about potential helpers or organisations where they can seek help.

### The 'Enquirer' Role

When a person is in the 'enquirer' role, they are making direct approaches to potential therapists or organisations offering therapeutic help. The 'enquiring' mindset is to find out more about therapeutic services directly and to discover what such services may cost. However, the person has not yet decided to seek help from any particular therapist or agency.

### The 'Applicant' Role

When a person is in the 'applicant' role, they have decided that they want to seek help from a particular therapist and agency and can thus be seen to have applied for such help. However, they cannot yet be appropriately considered to be a client.

### The 'Client' Role

When a person is in the client role, they have agreed with the therapist what service they are going to receive. They understand the nature of that service, together with its potential benefits and possible risks, and have decided to give their informed consent. At the point when they have given such consent, they can be said to become a client.

## The Pathway

When a person contacts me, usually by phone or by email, they are directly contacting me as I have no secretarial or administrative support. I undertake to give an immediate response to anybody making contact with me. In the case where somebody has left me their number, I call them back to discover whether they are in the 'enquirer' role or the 'applicant' role.

### Responding to Those in the 'Enquirer' Role

If a person is in the 'enquirer' role, I try to find out what questions they have to help them determine whether they wish to make an application to see me. This may result in my telling them what I charge or what services I offer in a general way. I may refer them to my website[1] for more information about the services that I offer, and if they would like more detailed information about SST, I send them an explanatory leaflet usually by email attachment (see Appendix 2).

### Responding to Those in the 'Applicant' Role

If a person is in the 'applicant' role, they may know that I offer SST and are clear that this is the kind of help that they seek, or they may not know about my SST service. If they are seeking SST, I ask them to tell me briefly why they think that this service may be particularly helpful to them. Unless it is very clear that they are looking for a very different service, I will go along with their wish to access SST help from me. I will also tell them a little about the way I work and, if they wish to proceed after this, I will send them an explanatory leaflet on SST if they want it (see Appendix 2) and a therapy contract to sign,

1  Please note that I refer to my work as ONEplus therapy on my website rather than SST for reasons that I discussed in Chapter 1.

date and return (see Appendix 3). Once I have received their signed and dated contract, I regard them as a client. I will then make an appointment to see them (either face-to-face or online) and then send them a pre-session questionnaire to complete and return before the session. The purpose of this form is to help them prepare for the session so that they get the most from it. It also helps me to understand what they are looking for (see Chapter 19).

With general applicants, my practice is to tell them about the range of services that I offer: SST, ongoing therapy, couples therapy and coaching, and then ask them which service would best meet their needs. If they nominate SST, I invite them to explain why and again I outline the way I work with SST (as above). If they wish to proceed with SST, as above, I send them my leaflet, if needed, and a therapy contract to sign, date and return, after which we make an appointment to have the session face-to-face or online. At this point I send them my pre-session questionnaire to complete and return (as above).

Chapter 18

# Contracting

## Abstract

Contracting involves the therapist and client agreeing to work
with one another based on a mutual understanding of the service that is on offer. I show how therapists might describe different forms of SST so that the client can give their informed
consent to proceed.

## Introduction

In the previous chapter, I outlined my own approach to contracting as it occurs in my independent practice. In this chapter,
I will discuss contracting for SST more generally as therapists
and agencies operate in different ways.

When the therapist and client meet for the SST session (either
face-to-face or online), it is vital for both to be clear about several important issues concerning their contract. In this chapter,
I will just focus on the nature of the service on offer to clients
and how a therapist might make this explicit. I will not discuss
other more general contract-related matters[1] such as an agency's
policy on confidentiality and risk assessment and management.

---

1  See Appendix 3 for how I word these aspects of the contract.

DOI: 10.4324/9781003413103-20

Here I will outline several different types of SST services and how they can be made explicit so that the client can give their informed consent to proceed, which becomes their contract. I will not discuss whether the contract should be in writing or agreed verbally as this is a more general therapeutic issue and pertains to all forms of service provision, not just SST issues. (My own practice is to work with a written contract in all the services I offer.)

## Only One Session

There are some SST therapists who only offer one session and some therapists who offer more but may be in a position to only offer one, for a variety of reasons. Typically, this has been discussed before the client comes to the session. For example, I was about to go on a business trip and, a few weeks before I left, someone rang me to see if they could book six sessions with me as they were visiting London for six weeks. Unfortunately, our diaries clashed and I was only able to offer the person one session, which they accepted. At the beginning of the session, I reminded the client that we had only one session, but that we could have Zoom sessions afterwards. However, she did not want to do that, so this was to be the only session we had apart from a follow-up to be arranged when she next was going to come to London.

When, for whatever reason, there is to be only one session, the therapist might say something like, 'As I discussed on the phone, we are only able to meet for one session, and you said that you were OK with that, but I just want to check with you that this is still the case'. If it is, the therapist can follow-up with, 'OK, so let's join forces and see if we as a team can help you take away something that will make a difference to you'.

## Open-Access, Enter Now Therapy

Open-access, enter now services offer people the opportunity to be seen promptly without an appointment. Some people use an open-access, enter now service once, while others may use it several times and different services have different stances concerning future sessions being available. Some state that a person may return while others say that, if a further session is needed, an appointment must be made (Dryden, 2019a). The critical point here is that the therapist should make it clear to the client what the policy of the service is before proceeding. Here is an example of what a therapist in one walk-in service might say:

> Before we start, I just want to make clear what the policy of this service is so that you can give the go ahead. Here, we offer one session and together we will focus on helping you with whatever you have come with. My wish is that we get the job done today, but if not and you want to return then that is possible, and you can come back in again. Is that clear? Do you have any questions? Shall we proceed on that basis?

## One Session with the Possibility of More

The current prevailing view in the SST community is that one session may be sufficient, but more sessions are available if needed. For example, a therapist may say something like:

> We have agreed to meet today, and if we both really focus we can help you to head in a direction that is right for you, and, if so, you may decide at the end that this is all that is needed. If not, further help is available. Shall we move forward on that basis?

## One-at-a-Time Therapy (OAATT)

OAATT is a therapy in which the person has one session at a time. Here the therapist says something like:

In this clinic, we offer one session at a time. So today, we will see if we can team up to address your problem to your satisfaction. At the end of the session, I will ask you to go away and reflect on what you have learned, digest it and then put it into practice. Then, after you have let things settle, if you decide that you need another session, please get back in touch, and you can book one. However, you can't book another session until two weeks have elapsed. If I have not helped you to your satisfaction today, you can book another session with me or one of my colleagues again in two weeks' time. How does that sound to you?

## Unique Features

If there are any features that are unique to the therapist's practice of SST, the therapist should make them clear at the outset and seek the client's agreement. For example, in my own practice of SST, I ask for permission to record the session. I state that part of the SST package that I offer involves me sending the client a digital voice recording of the session and, if requested, a written transcript of the recording for the client's later review. I make clear that while these are primarily for the benefit of the client, they also help me to reflect on my work and improve my service delivery (Dryden, 2022a).

# Chapter 19

# Preparing for the Session

## Abstract

In this chapter, I consider the issue of how best the therapist and client can prepare for the session so that the client can get the most from it. I cover both the context of such preparation and the content.

## Introduction

As every gardener knows, it is vital to prepare the ground before planting seeds. If this is not done, then weeds in the unprepared ground may impair the growth of these seeds with the result that the gardener will not get as much from the ground as they would do if it was adequately prepared.

This analogy applies to SST as well. The first (and perhaps only) session has a lot of potential benefits to be gained by the client. However, for these benefits to be realised, the therapist needs to work with the client to prepare for this session. Before I discuss the nature of this preparation, let me first review the contexts in which it can take place.

## Contexts for Session Preparation

Session preparation can take place in several contexts. Here I review some of the main contexts.

DOI: 10.4324/9781003413103-21

## Pre-Session Questionnaire

Many agencies that offer SST have a pre-session questionnaire for the client to complete and submit before they attend the session (see Table 19.1). Such a questionnaire can be completed on a physical form or online. The key points here are as follows:

- The client is told that the main purpose of the questionnaire is to help them to prepare for the session so that they can get the most from it.
- The client is informed that the completion of the questionnaire is advisory and not mandatory.
- The form is completed as close to the session as possible so that it reflects the client's current situation.
- The client is invited to return the form before the session so that the therapist can read the form and digest the information.

In open-access, enter now therapy clinics, the person can be asked to complete a brief pre-session questionnaire as there is generally a short wait before the person can be seen and this is an excellent way for the waiting time to be used.

## At the Beginning of the Session

It is possible for such preparation to take place in the session[1] itself. Here the therapist says that they would like to get vital information from the client before the session gets underway so

---

1 To be clear, by 'session', I mean any meeting in which the therapist and client can see or hear one another. This includes therapy where the two people are physically in the same room or over the internet. It also includes SST by telephone. While there is a growing practice where therapist and client interact over a text-based service, this falls outside of the remit of this book since the participants cannot see or hear one another.

*Table 19.1* The questions asked in one pre-session
questionnaire

I invite you to fill in this questionnaire before your
session with me. This will help you to prepare for the
session so that you can get the most from it. It also
helps me to help you as effectively as I can. Please
return it by email attachment before our session.
Please be brief and concise in your answers.

**Name:**                                          **Date:**

**1. What is the issue that you want to focus on in the
session?**
Be concise. In one or two sentences get to the heart of
the problem, if possible.

**2. Why is this significant?**
What's at stake? How does this affect your life? What is
the future impact if the issue is not resolved?

**3. What do you want to get from the session?**

**4. Specify briefly the relevant background
information.**
What you think I need to know about the issue to help
you with it? Summarise in bullet points.

*Table 19.1* (Continued)

---

**5. How have you tried to deal with the issue up to this point?**
What steps, successful or unsuccessful, have you taken so far in addressing the issue?

---

**6. What are the strengths or inner resources that you have as a person that you could draw upon while tackling the issue?**
If you struggle with answering this question, think of what people who really know you and who are on your side would say.

---

**7. Who are the people in your life who can support you as you tackle the issue?**
Name them and say what help each can provide.

---

**8. What help do you hope I can best provide you in the session? Please check the main one.**

☐ Help me to develop greater understanding of the issue
☐ Just listen while I talk about the issue
☐ Help me to express my feelings about the issue
☐ Help me to solve an emotional or behavioural problem; help me get unstuck
☐ Help me to make a decision
☐ Help me to resolve a dilemma
☐ Other (please specify):

Thank you.
Windy Dryden

that they can help the person get the most out of it. Note that a distinction is being made here between a period before the session starts and the session itself. This is best done when the contact between therapist and client is longer than usual (e.g. 90 minutes as opposed to 60 minutes). Again, the client is also invited to contribute to this process as an active partner.

## Content for Session Preparation

What does the therapist want to know when preparing for the session so that they can help the client get the most out of the session? While SST therapists will differ on this issue, what follows is a range of topics that might be included in the content of the pre-session preparation contact with suggestions of how they might be used in the session.[2]

* What are the reasons you are seeking help now?
* Who else is involved?
* How quickly do you want to be helped?
* What would you like to achieve by the end of the session?
* What previous attempts have you made to solve the problem and what was the outcome?

  * Utilise helpful attempts; discourage unhelpful attempts.

* How have you solved similar problems in the past?

  * Suggest transferring successful strategies to the problem.

* What relevant *strengths* do you have that you can bring to the process of SST?
* What *character virtues* do you have that will help you get the most from our work together?
* What important *values* do you have that might underpin our work?

2  Also, see Table 19.1 for an example of such content.

- How can I best help you when we have our face-to-face session?
- What *external resources* can you make use of that might be a benefit in therapy?
- What *music, literature and pieces of art* do you associate with effecting change?
- What *valuable lessons* has life taught you?
- What *principles of living* guide you?
- What *role models or influential figures* might encourage you to change in the way you want?

Again, let me stress that I am not advocating that the SST therapists ask their clients all of these questions. Preferably, they are to be used as a resource to select from, as appropriate.

# Chapter 20

# Getting Started

## Abstract

In this chapter, I consider different ways of beginning the single session once contracting has been done. Getting started is different if there has been a pre-session contact between therapist and client than if there has been no such contact, as will be shown.

## Introduction

After contracting has been done, the therapist and client are ready to begin the session. How the therapist begins the session depends, in part, on whether or not there has been any pre-session contact between them. In this chapter, I will consider both situations.

## Getting Started When the Client Has Completed the Pre-Session Questionnaire

When the client has completed and returned the pre-session questionnaire, here is an example of how to begin the session.

*Therapist:*    Thank you for completing the questionnaire. Would you mind if I refer to it during the session?

DOI: 10.4324/9781003413103-22

| | |
|---|---|
| *Client:* | No, that's fine. |
| *Therapist:* | What changes, if any, have you noticed sine you completed the questionnaire? |
| *Client:* | I have thought a bit about what I would like to get from the session. |
| *Therapist:* | What would you like to get from it? |
| *Client:* | Some 'tips' and 'techniques' to deal with my anxiety. |
| *Therapist:* | Do you think those are best selected once we understand your anxiety more fully or without such understanding? |
| *Client:* | I would have thought understanding my anxiety would be best. |
| *Therapist:* | So, in the session, shall we focus on understanding your anxiety with a view to finding some 'tips and techniques', as you call them, to deal with your anxiety? |
| *Client:* | Yes, that's fine. |

In this exchange, the therapist began by referencing the pre-session questionnaire and asking the client what changes they noticed after completing it. The client responded and the therapist used the client's response to begin the session and was able to create a focus for the session quite quickly.

Here is another way to begin the session with reference to the pre-session questionnaire.

| | |
|---|---|
| *Therapist:* | Thank you for completing the questionnaire. Would you mind if I refer to it during the session? |
| *Client:* | No, that's fine. |
| *Therapist:* | In response to the question on the form that asks 'What do you want to get from the session?', you said to deal with your stress at work. Is that still your goal? |
| *Client:* | Actually, no. Something specific happened at work yesterday that made me very upset, and I would like to deal with that. Is that OK? |

*Therapist:*    Of course, let's do that, and then we can see if there is anything you can take away from our discussion that will also help you more generally with your stress at work. Is that OK?

*Client:*    Fine.

In response to the therapist's query if their stated goal on the form was still current, the client said that it had changed. The therapist's response indicated that they would focus on the client's new topic, but built a potential bridge between that and the client's original goal.

### Getting Started When the Therapist Has Suggested a Pre-Session Task

Some therapists suggest that the client engages in a task between the initial contact (usually by phone or email) and the session. This is to build a bridge between the two contacts and either initiate a process of change or carry on such a process that has already been initiated by the client before they come to the session. In some contexts, it is not possible for therapists to suggest such tasks, but, when it is, it often bears fruit.

Two such suggestions that SST therapists typically make are what can be termed 'noticing' and 'doing' suggestions.

### When the Therapist Has Suggested a 'Noticing' Task

Talmon (1990: 19) gives one such example: 'Between now and our first session, I want you to notice the things that happen to you that you would like to keep happening to you in the future. In this way, you will help me to find out more about your goal and what you are up to'. At the beginning of the face-to-face session, the therapist might ask, 'What changes have you noticed since we spoke on the phone?' If the client reports a change, the therapist could ask:

- What did you do to bring about that change?
- What effect is that change having?
- If we had not spoken and made this change by the end of this session, how would you feel about making the change?

The client's responses suggest a way forward for the therapist regarding creating a possible focus for the session.

### When the Therapist Has Suggested a Behavioural Task

Sometimes during the pre-session contact, the client might mention something on the phone that lends itself to a suggestion by the therapist for the client to do something between that contact and the session. For example, When Harry spoke to me about the possibility of SST, he mentioned being anxious about the views of people older than him. Currently, he was anxious about his parents-in-law disapproving of him for wanting to move his family to a different part of the country. I asked him if he knew the viewpoint of his in-laws on this point? He said he did not, so I suggested that he find out before we had the session with the promise that I would help him deal with his feelings should they show disapproval. When we met for the session, I began by asking what happened when he told his in-laws of his plans:

*Windy:*　How did the discussion with your in-laws go?

*Harry:*　Much better than I thought.

*Windy:*　What happened?

*Harry:*　Well, I told them, and I was right. They did not like it. But, as we were talking, I realised that I did not mind about this as much as I thought I would. I also surprised myself that I stood up for myself and made the point that I would look after their daughter and that seemed to reassure them a bit. We left on better terms than I thought.

*Windy:*  What did you do to bring about this change?

*Harry:*  Well, you asked me to do it, but the main thing was that I decided to do it. When I made that decision, I noticed it calmed me down.

*Windy:*  So, deciding to take action is a good way to tackle anxiety.

*Harry:*  Yes.

*Windy:*  What else did you do to bring about change?

*Harry:*  I think standing up for myself was useful.

*Windy:*  So, taking a decision to act and standing up for yourself were key ingredients in this situation. Let's keep these at the forefront of our minds as we talk in the session. OK?

*Harry:*  OK.

*Windy:*  Can I share something with you?

*Harry:*  Sure.

*Windy:*  What struck me from what you said was that you spoke to them as an equal. I wonder what you think about that?

*Harry:*  [pause] ... Wow! That's spot on. With all these older people, I don't see myself as their equal.

*Windy:*  So that sounds like something we really need to focus on and link it to what you took from the experience. Does that make sense?

*Harry:*  Yes, it does.

This is a clear example of how in SST much can be gained from a simple suggestion and how the therapist uses the client's experience of the task to begin the session and almost immediately focus on a central theme. It also shows the importance of the therapist's expertise in sharing an observation that the client missed when he was reflecting on his own experience.

## Getting Started When There Has Been No Pre-Session Contact

When there has been no prior contact between the therapist and client before the session, as in open-access, enter now SST, the therapist can begin the session in the following ways:

### *Problem- and Solution-Focused SST*

When the therapist adopts a problem- and solution-focused approach, they might begin by asking the client:

- What problem do you have?
- If we were only going to meet once, what problem would you want to focus on solving at this point? (Haley, 1989)

### *Solution-Focused SST*

When taking a solution-focused approach, the therapist might ask:

- If you were to go home today and think that the session was worthwhile, what would have happened?
- What are you willing to change today? (Goulding & Goulding, 1979)
- What are your best hopes for today's meeting? (Iveson, George & Ratner, 2014)

In both cases, the client's answers allow the therapist to pick up the baton and use the responses to begin the process of change.

# Chapter 21

# Discovering What Help to Give

## Abstract

In this chapter, I will review the different types of help the SST therapist can offer in this mode of therapy delivery and make the point that it is important for the therapist to offer the help that the client is looking for and not what the therapist thinks the client needs.

## Introduction

It is commonly thought that SST was designed to help clients find solutions to existing emotional and/or behavioural problems. While the most common form of help that clients seek from SST is emotional/behavioural problem-solving, this is by no means the only type of help that clients seek from SST. Before I briefly list the different types of help that are available in SST, I want to make the point that what is crucial is that the therapist offers the client the help that the client wants not what the therapist thinks the client needs. When the therapist meets the client's SST helping preferences, this strengthens their working alliance and has a positive impact on what the client takes from SST (Norcross & Cooper, 2021).

The following are the most common types of help that clients seek from SST:

DOI: 10.4324/9781003413103-23

- Help me to solve an emotional or behavioural problem and get unstuck.
- Help me to develop a greater understanding of an issue.
- Help me to express my feelings about an issue and get things off my chest.
- Just listen while I talk about an issue.
- Just let me talk about whatever I want to talk about. Don't try to focus me.
- Help me make a decision.
- Help me resolve a dilemma.
- Give me your professional opinion on something.
- Signpost me to appropriate services.

While it is important to take the client's help-seeking preference at face value, sometimes it is useful to understand if there is an unexpressed link in the client's mind about different types of help. Therefore, it is useful for the therapist to look for such a link. Here is an example:

*Windy:*   What help are you looking for from me today?
*Client:*   Well, I'd like to get a deeper understanding about why I get anxious because it is not clear to me.
*Windy:*   What do you think getting such understanding will do for you?
*Client:*   It will help me to deal with my anxiety better. That's what I really hope to get from today.
*Windy:*   So, it sounds like we need to begin by trying to figure out together why you get anxious and then, on the basis of that understanding, we should try to help you to deal better with your anxiety. Is that right?
*Client:*   Yes.

In this example, the unexpressed link in the client's mind was that getting a deeper understanding of their anxiety would help them to deal with it better.

It is not always the case that the client's stated helping preference is linked to other forms of help, as is shown in the following example:

*Windy:*   What help are you looking for from me today?
*Client:*   Well, I'd like to express my feelings about what is going on at home.
*Windy:*   What do you think expressing your feelings will do for you?
*Client:*   I just find it useful to express my feelings with someone who is not directly involved in my life.
*Windy:*   I am happy to help you do that. Where would you like to start?

In this example, the client wanted to express her feelings and did not have any other form of help in mind.

The point to keep in mind here is that, if the SST therapist does not enquire about the possible existence of an unexpressed link, then they may not provide the help that the client really wants but has not expressed. However, as the above example shows, the client may only want the type of help first expressed.

In the rest of the book, I will assume that the client wants the most frequently requested type of help from SST, which is 'Help me to solve an emotional or behavioural problem and get unstuck'.

Chapter 22

# Working with Problems and Goals

## Abstract

SST therapists differ concerning what issues they attend to during the single session. Some attend to problems, goals and solutions, while others attend to goals and solutions. It is unlikely that there are too many SST therapists working with clients' problems alone without reference to goals and solutions. In this chapter, I consider how SST therapists can work with problems and goals and will consider how they work with solutions in Chapter 27.

## Introduction

When a client comes to therapy, it is usually because they are in some kind of problematic state and are looking for help with that state. This state is typically called a 'problem'. What the client hopes to achieve from therapy is to arrive at or return to a non-problematic state. This state is typically called a 'goal'. A 'solution' is a means of addressing the problem that moves the person closer to their goal. In my training workshops, I use a simple diagram to illustrate this, which I reproduce in Figure 22.1 (see also Chapter 13). This figure shows that the therapist begins by focusing on the problem, then helps the client to set a goal that is related to the problem and that influences the negotiation of a solution. The client often says that they

DOI: 10.4324/9781003413103-24

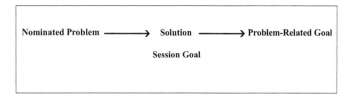

*Figure 22.1* The relationship between problems, solutions and goals

want to find a solution by the end of the session, which explains why a session goal is often a solution. The client then implements the negotiated solution, which takes them closer towards their problem-related goal. Note then the distinction between a session goal and a problem-related goal.

In this chapter, I will discuss how SST therapists work with problems and goals since these are therapists' tasks that are closer to the beginning of the session. Since working with solutions comes later, I will consider them later in this book (see Chapter 26).

Before I start, I want to make the point that some SST therapists tend only to work with goals and solutions (e.g. solution-focused therapists). Such therapists tend to see working with problems as focusing on the negative and on what is *wrong* with the client. By working with goals and solutions, such therapists consider that they are working with the realistically positive and focusing on what is *right* with the client. Other SST therapists argue that, as clients expect to talk about their problems, a certain amount of focused time can usefully be spent in SST on doing so since this can reveal what the client has a problem with and how they unwittingly maintain the problem. Of course, these SST therapists also work with goals and solutions.

## Working with the Problem

When working with the client's problem, it is vital that the therapist does this in a way that conveys to the client that the problem is solvable. There are two components of working with a problem: (i) identifying the problem and (ii) assessing its main features.

### Identifying the Problem

A client may come to SST with a number of problems. When this is the case, as there is probably only time for therapist and client to deal with one, the therapist needs to help the client to select one. Here are a number of questions that the therapist can ask when identifying the client's problem for SST:

- What problem do you want to solve today?
- Imagine that, when you get home today, we have successfully worked together to solve one of your problems. What problem would you want us to have solved?
- Of these problems, which one is it most important for you to solve?
- If we tackled one of your problems successfully today, which one would give you the sense that you have made a significant step forward?

As shown in Figure 22.1, I refer to the problem that the client wants to discuss in the session as the 'nominated problem'.

### Assessing the Nominated Problem

Once the client has nominated a problem to focus on, the next stage is for the therapist to help the client to assess the problem. Such an assessment is going to depend, in part, on the professional constructs that the therapist uses to make sense of such problems, and in part on the client's view of this issue.

In my single-session practice, I am keen to understand the main adversity that features in the client's problem, their main problematic emotion, unconstructive behaviour and highly distorted thinking. Also, I am interested to learn about the contribution that any significant others make to the problem.

## Negotiating a Goal

Usually, the client's goal relates to their problem. However, as solution-focused therapists (e.g. Ratner, George & Iveson, 2012) note, a therapist can negotiate goals with the client without reference to the client's problem.

### Negotiating a Goal Related to the Client's Problem

When the SST therapist is negotiating a goal with a client related to that person's nominated problem, my view is that the achievement of the goal needs to be realistic. Thus, if the client's problem is anxiety about being judged negatively by others in a social situation and the client nominates a goal that involves being confident in such social situations, such a goal is realistic if it rests on the person first dealing productively with negative judgments from others. If it is not, and the client wants to bypass dealing with such judgments, then in my view this is unrealistic as it is difficult to develop social confidence when one is anxious about being negatively judged by others. Here, the therapist's task is to help the client to understand this and to nominate 'dealing productively with adverse social judgment' as their general goal for SST, which is then spelt out. This example points to the distinction between 'dealing with problem' goals and 'enhancing development' goals. A good rule is: negotiate and help the client pursue the former before you accept and help them to pursue the latter (Dryden, 2018b).

Here, the therapist might ask:

- 'What goal would you like to achieve concerning your problem?' This is known as a problem-related (or outcome) goal and the client needs to understand that this is most likely to be achieved after the session.
- When a client sets a problem-related, outcome goal, the SST therapist might ask, 'If I helped you today to take one step that would give you a sense that you were on the way to achieving your goal, what would that step be?' This can be seen as a process goal and is a more constructive goal for SST than a problem-related, outcome goal. For this reason, it is often referred to as a session goal since the client is being asked to nominate a goal to be achieved by the end of the session.
- Session goals are probably the favoured goal of SST therapists.

### Negotiating a Goal without Reference to the Client's Problem

Here, given that the therapist is seeking to negotiate a goal without reference to the client's problem, goal-setting questions can be used to kick-off the SST process as we have seen in the previous chapter. For example, I mentioned in that chapter the question suggested by Iveson, George & Ratner (2014), 'What are your best hopes for today's meeting?', which can be seen as a session goal. Another session goal has been suggested by Talmon (1993: 40)

- 'What would you like to accomplish today?'

### SMART Goals

Whether goals are negotiated related to problems or not, it is a good idea if they are 'SMART'. This is an acronym that stands for:

**'S' = Specific.** Specific goals should be clear enough to help the client see for what they are aiming.

**'M' = Motivating.** While 'M' usually stands for 'measurable', my view is that 'motivating' is more useful for SST, particularly if it makes clear what the reasons are for change.

**'A' = Achievable.** Only achievable goals have a place in SST.

**'R' = Relevant.** The goal needs to be relevant to the client's life if they are to work to achieve it.

**'T' = Time-bound.** It is important that the goal can be achieved in a specified period of time. What is most important is that, if the goal can't be achieved by the end of the session, then the client can see where they are heading and can use their strengths to get there after therapy has ended.

# Chapter 23

# Creating and Maintaining a Session Focus

## Abstract

In this chapter, I point out that the therapist needs to co-create a focus with the client. This focus will often be related to the client's problem, goal and solution, or related just to the goal and solution. I discuss the natural human tendency to wander away from a focus, especially in conversations, and argue that polite, respectful interruption is what the therapist should do if the client departs from the agreed session focus. I then consider why therapists may have difficulty interrupting their clients and what they need to do about it. I conclude by considering what to do if the client departs from an agreed focus by not answering the therapist's key questions.

## Introduction

Once the client and therapist have begun work, their next task is to co-create a focus for the session. This focus may have several components. It will most often comprise a problem, a goal and a solution, as mentioned in the previous chapter, or merely a goal and a solution.

As I made clear in Chapter 13 on the working alliance, it is crucial for the therapist and client to agree on their view of the problem, the client's goals and what constitutes an acceptable solution. Consequently, it is useful for the therapist to check

DOI: 10.4324/9781003413103-25

periodically that the focus is still an agreed one. It may need to be modified as the session unfolds, but, if it is modified too often, this is not a good sign.

## The Natural Human Tendency to Wander and Become Distracted

Most human beings find it difficult to stay focused on a task even if the task and the goal that it leads to are meaningful to them. Our minds wander, and it is a fundamental rule of meditation that, when a person is focusing on their mantra, other thoughts will come into their mind. The person is advised to accept the presence of these thoughts and then go back to focusing on their mantra.

This process also happens in conversation. In social communication, people range over a number of topics, with one topic stimulating another as two people enjoy each other's company. Even in a purposeful conversation, where the goal is to discuss one topic and come to a conclusion, people still get distracted and wander away from the focus. SST is one such purposive conversation and therefore, given that some clients will find it easier to stay focused than others, the therapist needs to be able to help those who find it difficult to create and maintain the focus.

Clients wander away from the agreed session focus in two ways. First, they provide too much information for the purposes of SST about the contexts in which their problem occurred, and second, they move away from the specific to the general when it is crucial for them to focus on the specific. In the first situation, the person needs to be helped to provide only the information that will help the dyad to address and solve the problem together. In the second situation, the client needs to be brought back to the specific context. This is primarily done in two ways. First, the therapist checks with the client if the two are still on track, and second, the therapist needs to interrupt the client but do so politely and respectfully.

## Polite, Respectful Interruption

There are a number of issues that need to be addressed concerning interrupting clients, a task with which many therapists struggle.

### Provide a Rationale for Interrupting the Client

One way of making it easier to interrupt the client is to provide them with a rationale for doing so. I usually say something like:

> To get the most from sessions like this, it is important that you and I both stay focused on your goal. Some people find it hard to stay focused and, without realising it, they wander from the agreed topic at hand. If that happens with us, may I have your permission to interrupt you and bring you back to the focus?

### Ask for and Obtain the Client's Permission to Interrupt

Once the rationale has been provided, it is crucial for the therapist to ask the client for their permission to interrupt them. Thus, as shown above, you can say, 'If that happens with us, may I have your permission to interrupt you and bring you back to the focus?' Clients who have a problem with staying focused generally recognise this and are relieved when the therapist offers to interrupt them and thus readily give their permission.

### When the Therapist Has a Problem with Interrupting Clients

The difficulties therapists have with interrupting their clients tend to be twofold. First, many therapists think that it is essential to facilitate the client's self-exploration and that to interrupt their 'flow' is counterproductive even when the clients wander from issue to issue. This viewpoint is unhelpful in SST, where the focus is on one issue rather than allowing the client to take the lead in opening the conversation up in a broader way.

Second, some therapists think that interrupting clients is rude. My response is that it can be rude to do so if the therapist does it rudely. However, if the therapist does it tactfully after giving the client a rationale and gaining their permission, then this does not constitute rude practice. It constitutes good practice in SST.

### Ensure That the Client Answers Important Questions or Change Tack

If the SST therapist asks the client a vital question within the created session focus, and the client does not answer the question, then the therapist needs to bring this to the client's attention and invite the client to give an answer. If the client continues not to answer the question, the therapist needs to inquire about the reason. The client's response needs to be considered within the SST time constraints and the therapist needs to makes a judgment call concerning whether or not to proceed with the question given these constraints. If a different tack can be taken to help the client find a solution, then it should be taken. Flexibility is key here as elsewhere in the SST process.

Chapter 24

# Doing the Work

## Abstract

In this chapter, I discuss what SST therapists tend to do in the
middle phase of the process, which, as Hoyt (2000) notes, concerns refocus and change. I frame my discussion by showing
what work therapists from the three major single-session traditions tend to do in this phase.

## Introduction

What the therapist and client do, having created a session
focus, is going to depend, in large part, on their view of how
best to facilitate client change in the session. As I discussed in
Chapter 5, there is no one SST approach. Instead, it is a mindset
that the therapist brings to the process, and this mindset can be
applied by therapists guided by a variety of therapeutic ideas
and orientations. The common thread is that the therapist draws
upon a range of client variables and encourages the client to
use them while searching for a solution to solve their problem
and achieve their goal or to take a key first step in that process,
which they can continue on their own after the session. The
diverse thread is, as I have said, that therapists bring a plethora
of different ways of doing this. This is why I have called this
chapter, 'Doing the work', to indicate such diversity.

DOI: 10.4324/9781003413103-26

The client also has to 'do the work' by contributing their own views on what will help them bring about change, and by sharing what they have found helpful and unhelpful in dealing with this and related problems beforehand.

## Doing the Work: Three SST Traditions

A therapeutic tradition is comprised of a number of specific therapeutic approaches that subscribe to a coherent set of ideas that influence practice. These approaches may have differences that may be barely observable to the outsider, but may be very important to the insider.[1] Elsewhere, I have used the terms 'constructive', 'active-directive' and 'pluralistic' as labels to describe the three major therapeutic traditions (Dryden, 2019a). In this chapter, I will give a flavour of how SST therapists from these three traditions do the work in the middle phase of the single session.

### The 'Constructive' Tradition

Hoyt et al. (2018b: 14) state that approaches within the constructive SST tradition are 'non-pathologising, solution-focused, collaborative or narrative' in nature. Therapists from this tradition use their expertise to help clients to utilise their own, often overlooked or disregarded, expertise in discovering and implementing solutions to their problems. What such therapists tend not to do is focus on problems or offer the client a perspective on their problems and how to address them or on how to best choose their solutions and/or reach their goals. Therapists from this tradition are decidedly client-centred (Dryden, 2024). Here is a sample of how constructive therapists tend to do the work in the middle phase of SST.

1  As an example of this, see Gonzalez, Estrada & O'Hanlon (2011) on the differences between solution-focused therapy and solution-oriented therapy. Partly to distinguish itself from solution-focused therapy, O'Hanlon changed the name of solution-oriented therapy to possibility therapy.

*Identifying exceptions.* Here, the therapist encourages the client to look for exceptions to the problem and focuses their attention on what they did to make the problem a 'non-problem'. Once such client-enacted strategies have been identified, the therapist works with the client to enable them to initiate and develop them (see Ratner et al., 2012).

*Identifying instances of the goal already happening.* As can be seen from the above, identifying exceptions does involve keeping the problem in the frame. Partly for this reason, practitioners of solution-focused therapy moved away from this method to one that is more in keeping with the philosophy of solution-focused therapy. This involves encouraging the client to identify instances when the person reached their goal. Once identified, the therapist helps the client to identify what it was that they did to achieve their goal, and once found the therapist encourages the client, as above, to use such strategies in the future.

*Identifying and transferring overlooked helpful strategies from other areas.* I once worked with a client (not in SST) who had a problem with criticism. I helped him to deal with his anxiety of being criticised by his boss in one session and in the next session he presented with anxiety about being criticised by his mother-in-law. When I asked him if he had put into practice what he had learned from our successful discussion about how to deal with his anxiety about his boss's criticism, since the factors were almost identical, he replied, 'No, I didn't. It did not occur to me. If I knew I could do it then I would have done so'. This taught me an excellent lesson. Left to their own devices, many clients are not good at self-generated transfer of learning from one context to another. Such generalisation needs to be built into the therapy process. This is what constructive therapists do. They search for strategies that clients have used to solve other problems and help them to see which of these strategies they could use to achieve their problem-related goal.

### The 'Active-Directive' Tradition

In my view, therapists from an 'active-directive' tradition in SST differ from therapists in the 'constructive' tradition in that they are more likely to work with problems than their constructive colleagues and they bring to the process their views about how people develop and maintain problems and how they can address these problems effectively. However, in the spirit of collaboration and with due regard to the working alliance (see Chapter 13), such therapists do two things that I will discuss more fully in the section on the pluralistic tradition. First, they ask their clients for permission to give their views about the problem and how it may be addressed. Second, they invite the use of a range of client factors.

Hoyt et al. (2018b) gave the following examples of active-directive approaches to SST: REBT/CBT, redecision/Gestalt, psychodynamic, and some forms of strategic therapy. In my view, there are many more differences in the content of ideas among active-directive approaches than there are among constructive approaches. Given this, let me outline what I tend to do in the middle phase of the single session as a representative of REBT/CBT within the active-directive tradition (see Dryden, 2018a, 2022a).

*My practice: Problem assessment.* When the client and I agree which problem we are going to focus on, I will assess the problem using the 'ABC' framework of REBT, which I will only present if I have the client's permission to do so. I stress that this is one way of making sense of their problem, not the only way, and I am interested in their view about this and their own understanding of the factors involved in the problem and its maintenance. In working with the problem, I will ask the client for an example of it. This can be recent, vivid, typical or anticipated. I find it particularly useful to work with an anticipated example of the problem since it is easier for a client to apply learning to the same situation that we have chosen to work with (i.e. anticipated) than it is to take what they have learned from an assessment of a past example and apply it to an anticipated example. I will offer this rationale to the client. However, ultimately, I will go along with the client's choice on this matter.

In the 'ABC' framework, 'A' stands for the main _A_dversity that features in the client's problem, 'B' stands for the _B_asic rigid and extreme attitudes that the person holds towards the adversity and 'C' stands for the emotional, behavioural and cognitive _C_onsequences of holding the basic attitudes. I usually assess them in the order 'C', 'A', 'B'. Since the work goes much better when I have identified the client's adversity correctly, I often spend quite a bit of time identifying 'A' precisely (as shown in Dryden. 2018a).

*Setting adversity-related goals.* While I may have asked for the client's goal for the session earlier on in the session, it is vital for me to ask them for their goal in handling the adversity once I have discovered it. I would describe my practice of SST as adversity focused in that, if I can help the person deal effectively with the identified adversity, or to take a significant step towards doing so, then I think that I have achieved my goal as an SST therapist.

*My practice: Helping people to begin the attitude change process.* I do not expect my client to have changed their attitude at the end of the first, and perhaps the only, session that they have with me. However, I can help them to take the first step towards it, and it is surprising how much long-term benefit people have derived from doing so (see Dryden, 2018a). There are a number of ways of facilitating attitude change in SST, and I refer the reader to Dryden (2022a) and Dryden (2018a).

I will return to other aspects of my single-session practice in several of the following chapters.

### The 'Pluralistic' Tradition

The following are several pluralistic principles that are relevant to SST (taken from Dryden, 2019a, 114–115).

- There is no one absolute right way of understanding clients' problems and solutions – different viewpoints are useful for different clients.
- There is no one absolute right way of practising SST – different clients need different things, and therefore SST therapists need to have a broad practice repertoire.
- Disputes and disagreements in the SST field may, in part, be able to be resolved by taking a 'both-and' perspective, rather than an 'either/or' one.
- It is important that SST therapists respect each other's work and recognise the value that it can have.
- SST therapists should ideally acknowledge and celebrate clients' diversity and uniqueness.
- Clients should ideally be involved fully throughout the SST process.
- Clients should ideally be understood in terms of their strengths and resources as well as their areas of struggle.
- SST therapists should ideally have an openness to multiple sources of knowledge on how to practise SST: including research, personal experience and theory.
- It is important that SST therapists take a critical perspective on their own theory and practice: being willing to look at their own investment in a particular position and having the ability to stand back from it.

The above distinction between constructive and active-directive approaches is rather black and white, and the reality is probably less clear-cut. Thus, while I would probably place myself more in the 'active-directive' camp than in the 'constructive' camp, I do two things that might be more closely allied with 'constructive' practice in SST. First, I ask my clients if they would be interested in my view of their problem and how we might address it and only proceed when they agree to do so. In doing so, I would seek their views on these two points and would incorporate these views into our joint work.

Second, I would *also* actively identify and use the client factors that I identified in the pre-session contact that were relevant to the problem that my client and I were working on. So, while I would self-identify as an active-directive SST therapist, I am also influenced and guided by 'constructive' SST principles.

Moshe Talmon who, I would say, is more in the constructive SST camp than the active-directive camp, has given good examples of the pluralistic nature of his SST practice (Talmon, 2018: 153). Thus, in working with clients, the therapist may at different times in the same session:

- Validate a client's story via empathic listening and challenge the problematic elements in the same storyline.
- Increase a sense of hope or a realistic sense of optimism, and help a person to accept certain parts of the harsh reality.
- Offer neutral (and at times passive, silent) listening in one part of a session and, in another part, present active, focused questions.
- The therapist should be non-directive at one point of the session, and at other times give prescriptive-like directions.

As the field of SST matures, I hope that therapists in the constructive and active-directive traditions will learn to appreciate and incorporate each other's strengths into their work in the same way as they identify and incorporate their clients' strengths. When this happens, perhaps a pluralistic practice will be predominant in the field of SST.

# Chapter 25

# Utilising Client Variables

## Abstract

In this chapter, I focus on how SST therapists use client variables in the session in the service of the client's change process. I give examples showing the questions that a therapist can ask when using a client's strengths, their previous attempts to solve the problem and their role models in dealing with their problem and/or in the service of their goal.

## Introduction

Single-session work is in large part based on the principle of client empowerment. The view is that the client has lost their way in life or has got stuck and has also lost touch with the strong and resilient parts of themselves. The therapist's primary task is to help the client to reconnect with those constructive parts of self and to see that they can be applied to help achieve their goal or to get unstuck. As I discussed in Chapter 19, if SST is by appointment, the therapist gives the client an opportunity to prepare themself for the session work together so that the client gets the most from the session. If SST is offered by an open-access, enter now service, however, the therapist needs to identify growthful client variables as the single session unfolds, 'on the hoof', as it were.

DOI: 10.4324/9781003413103-27

*Table 25.1* Important client variables in SST

- Internal strengths
- Values
- Previous attempts to solve the problem
- Successful attempts to deal with other problems
- Helping others
- Being helped by others
- Role models
- Guiding principles
- External resources

In Chapter 7, I considered what these client variables might be, and these are listed in Table 25.1 as an aide-memoire so that readers can refer to it in this chapter.

Here are some examples of how to use client variables in SST.

## Using Internal Strengths

- Which of the strengths that you listed on your pre-session questionnaire might help you to speak up when your boss tries to take advantage of you?

If a client cannot remember their nominated strengths then the therapist can prompt as follows:

- You mentioned that persistence and the ability to understand people from their point of view are two of your main strengths. Would either or both of these help you to speak up to your boss?
- Referring to your pre-session questionnaire, here is the list of your expressed strengths. Which of these strengths would help you to stand up to your boss?

When the client nominates a particular strength, the therapist could ask questions such as:

- 'So, understanding people from their point of view is the strength that will help you the most to speak up to your boss if he tries to take advantage of you. How will you use that strength in the situation?'

It is useful to help clients take the generality of a particular strength and help them to specify how they would use it in a concrete situation.

## Using Previous Attempts to Solve the Problem

Here is a dialogue between myself as therapist and a client that shows how a therapist can use the client's previous attempts to solve the problem to shape a better solution. Here the client is struggling with social anxiety when out on dates.

*Windy:*    You mentioned a few things that you tried in the past that weren't helpful to you, like having a list of pre-pared topics to talk about and asking about hobbies. Why do you think that these were not helpful to you?

*Jean:*    Well they just came over as very trite.

*Windy:*    And you mentioned asking open-ended questions about what the other person was really interested in was the one thing you tried that was helpful. What was helpful about that?

*Jane:*    Well, initially it took the focus off of me, but, as the person started talking and I showed genuine interest, he seemed to light up, and then he asked me about my interests, and we had a good conversation.

*Windy:*    So, what was the difference between the two strategies?

*Jane:*    The first was something I wasn't really interested in, but the second I was.

*Windy:*    So, how can you use this insight to help you deal with your fear of dating?

*Jane:*    To be genuinely interested in the other person.

*Windy:*    And how can you do that?

*Jane:*    By inviting them to talk about something that they are really into.

Note that, in this segment, my interventions were mainly open-ended. I first asked the person to describe what they had tried that had not been helpful to them and then to describe what they had tried that had been helpful. Then I asked them what was different between the two strategies rather than offer my interpretation, which I would have done if my open-ended approach did not bear fruit. I then invited them to think of how they could put their self-derived insight into practice.

## Using Nominated Role Models

Here is another dialogue that I had with a client where I used one of the client's role models to good effect. The client could not think of having had any success with past attempts to solve their problem, which was feeling guilty about saying no to his mother when she made unreasonable requests of him.

*Windy:*    So, nothing that you have tried before has been helpful, even a little?

*Jerry:*    Not really. Alcohol helps in the short term, but I really don't want to go down that route.

*Windy:*    I get that. Do you recall that on your pre-session questionnaire, there was a question about who your role models are?

*Jerry:*    Yes, I do. I mentioned three, I believe.

*Windy:* Which of the three people you mentioned would have been able to solve the problem after grappling with it? *[Notice that I introduce the idea of solving the problem after grappling with it. I find that the most influential role models are those who struggle with and then overcome a problem. There needs to be a foundation of realism here.]*

*Jerry:* My cousin, Raphael.

*Windy:* What makes you say that?

*Jerry:* Well, he has had similar problems with his mother but has managed to say 'no'.

*Windy:* How do you think he managed that?

*Jerry:* Well, knowing him, he would say 'no' to his mother and explain why. If she made unreasonable requests of him, I would see him roll his eyes to himself, but reiterate why he was not going to do what she requested.

*Windy:* What would he do or think not to feel guilty?

*Jerry:* I think he would remind himself that he is a good son and that, if his mother was upset, that was unfortunate, but it wasn't going to stop him from standing his ground.

*Windy:* OK. What can you learn from him?

*Jerry:* That if I am clear and kind… because Raphael is kind, I will know in my own mind that I am a good son and, when my mother implies or tells me that I am not, I can see her behaviour for what it really is, an attempt to control me.

*Windy:* Can you imagine putting that perspective into practice?

*Jerry:* I think so.

I then went on to encourage Jerry to practise this solution with me in the session (see Chapter 28).

# Chapter 26

# Making an Impact

## Abstract

In this chapter, I show how to increase the impact that a session may have on a client in SST. However, first, I discuss several 'red flags' where the therapist needs to tread carefully when considering increasing the impact of their SST work.

## Introduction

There are a number of principles in SST as I have made clear in this book. These can be expressed in pithy phrases such as:

* *'More haste, less speed'*, which sums up the idea that, when an SST therapist rushes, they often make less progress than if they work at a steady pace.
* *'Sooner is better'*, which sums up the idea that when clients are seen quickly with a single session, they often do better than if they are placed on a lengthy waiting list for more sessions.
* *'More is less'*, which sums up the recognition that, when the SST therapist tries to cover much ground in a session and wants the client to take away a lot, this is frequently less effective than if they take away one meaningful point that they can implement immediately.

DOI: 10.4324/9781003413103-28

I maintain that such pithy phrases make the principles more memorable and thus have more impact on trainee SST therapists than if the more wordy versions of the principles were used. This is the main point of this chapter. If the therapist increases the impact of the single session, the client is more likely to benefit from the session than if it lacked impact.

## First, a Few Red Flags

I think that I can make this chapter more impactful if I first spell out a few words of warning.

### Less Is More

It is crucial that the client is not overloaded with the therapist's smart 'impactful' interventions. If the client can take away one impactful point that has meaning for them, this is better than several points of impact, most of which would soon be forgotten, probably including the one that had the most impact on them.

### Don't Emotionally Overstimulate a Client

A good SST session engages the client's emotions so that they can feel and process at the same time. Too much emotion and they stop thinking. Too little emotion and both therapist and client will have an interesting, but unproductive, theoretical discussion.

### Don't Push for Impact

The more an SST therapist deliberately pushes for impact, the less likely it is to happen. This is another version of the 'more is less' principle.

### Don't Copy Other Therapists' Techniques

While there are some techniques that are often used in SST (see Dryden, 2024), when it comes to techniques that will make an impact on a particular client, it is best not to use other therapists' techniques. On this point, 'made to measure' is better than 'off the peg'.

### You Never Know What Will Have an Impact on the Client

For me, one of the exciting things about being an SST therapist is that I never know what is going to happen. I may think that something will have an impact on a client, but it does not. Conversely, something will have an impact on a client that I could never predict. It is crucial that this not deter therapists from working with impact.

## Ways of Increasing the Impact of Single Sessions

With the above caveats in mind, here are a number of ways that SST therapists can increase the impact of their work with clients.

### Understand the Nuances of a Client's Emotions

When a client feels understood by the therapist and the nuances of their emotions attended to, they can search for a solution with an appropriate level of emotional engagement.

### Use One's Voice and Gestures for Emphasis

I have seen and heard many therapy sessions carried out by therapists who talk with little expression and sit very still.

While this may be appropriate in some circumstances, it will not necessarily make an impact on the client. I tend to vary my tone quite a bit doing therapy and use my hands quite a bit. In particular, I sometimes use my voice in the same way as I use a highlighter – to emphasise particular points.

### Use the Client's Own Words

When clients use certain words in referring to troublesome experiences, it is crucial that the therapist uses the same words rather than synonyms or vague terms like 'it', which lessens the impact of the therapist's later interventions.

### Identify and Work with the Client's Imagery

Working with a client's emotion-infused imagery can be particularly powerful. The key point is that the therapist needs to ask about imagery to work with it as clients do not always mention it without being asked.

### Use Self-Disclosure

Therapist self-disclosure can have a profound impact on one client and leave another one cold. There are two critical points for therapists to keep in mind: (i) ask the client for permission before disclosing an experience and (ii) only share experiences where struggle preceded triumph and show the pathway from the former to the latter.

### Employ Visual Techniques

Visual methods can be memorable and therefore impactful. For example, I was working with a client on a weight issue when she discussed being at a party and having no control over her hand, which scooped up food. I asked her to show me what her hand did, and then I did it, which she found very funny, and it was an image that she subsequently used in dealing with her food-related impulses.

## Use Humour

Humour can be an effective way of increasing impact as long as the therapist has a good sense of humour and the client responds well to it. Training therapists to use their humour is possible. Training them to be humorous is probably not.

## Show Relevant 'YouTube' Videos

There is a YouTube video that is pertinent to the practice of SST.[1] It shows in an impactful way the importance of doing something different, a point that it is vital for many SST clients to learn as they keep doing the same old thing and keep getting the same old results. But how best to help them grasp this point? I have found a YouTube video that gets the point across beautifully.

A father is encouraging his very young daughter to count to '5'. She says, '1,2,3,5'. Naturally, the father corrects her, 'No sweetie; it's 1,2,3,4,5', said with mild emphasis. 'No daddy', replies the little girl, 'it's 1,2,3,5'. The father corrects her as before, and his daughter responds as before. After several rounds of this same interaction, with the father using the fingers of his hand to stress the missing '4', with verbal emphasis of the '*4*' in his '1,2,3,*4*,5', the increasingly exasperated father appeals to his authority. 'Listen, sweetie; I teach this stuff every day. I'm a teacher. It's "1,2,3,*4*,5"', said with great emphasis. His daughter responds with equal emphasis, '*No!* It's 1,2,3,5'. At this point the father walks away, shaking his head, admitting defeat. Then, the mother enters the situation. 'Sweetie, your

---

1   www.youtube.com/watch?v=ZtUPKekDY7M ('Little Girl Argues with Dad About Counting', Jukin Media, accessed 19 March 2023).

father is right, It's 1,2,3,4,5'. 'No, mommy, it's 1,2,3,5'. After a few rounds of this, the mother changes tack. 'Sweetie, count to "4"'. The daughter thinks for a moment and says, '1,2,3,4'. At this point, one can see on the video that the daughter has just had a light bulb moment. She now sees that '4' comes before '5'.

What this delightful video shows us is how humans can perpetuate their problems by getting locked into stuck patterns. It also shows us that we can bring about change quite quickly when we do something different that breaks the impasse. I sometimes recommend that my client views this video, when it is relevant to their experience, since its impact is more significant than anything that I can say to them on the importance of doing something different when what they are doing is not working.

### Stories, Parables and Metaphors

Telling an appropriate story or parable or using an apt metaphor can have quite an impact on the client. I tell the following story to clients who claim that people don't listen to them and whose problems are rooted in their failure to be heard.

> A farmer had a donkey that did everything that it was asked. When told to work, the donkey worked. When told to stop, the donkey stopped. And when told to eat, the donkey ate. One day the farmer sold the donkey to his neighbour. He told his neighbour that all he had to say to the donkey was 'Come on donkey, sweet, sweet donkey, let's go to work', for example, and the donkey would obey his order. After settling the donkey into his new shed for a few days, the new owner excitedly went into the shed and said, 'Come on donkey, sweet, sweet donkey, let's go to work'. But the donkey did not move. The same happened the next morning and the next. Vexed, the new owner went to the farmer to get his money back. The farmer was puzzled and said that he would

come over the next morning to investigate. The next morning the farmer came into the donkey shed with his neighbour, looked around, picked up a two by four plank of wood, whacked the donkey on its nose with it and said, 'Come on donkey, sweet, sweet donkey, let's go to work', and the donkey started work. Amazed the new owner enquired as to the farmer's method. 'I'm awfully sorry', said the farmer, 'I forgot to tell you one important thing. You have to get its attention first!'

The client usually gets the point, which is that they have been communicating with someone without first getting their full attention. This usually leads to a discussion of ways to get a person's attention before you start communicating with them.

# Chapter 27

# Negotiating a Solution

## Abstract

In this chapter, I consider several issues concerning negotiating a solution with a client. I first offer an SST-based definition of a solution. Then, I distinguish between a chosen solution and a potential solution before discussing what insights working alliance theory have to offer the process of negotiating a solution. I end by outlining some of the main types of solution clients can be helped to choose and implement.

## Introduction

Dictionary definitions of the word 'solution' tend to refer to a problem rather than a goal. For example, the *Oxford English Dictionary* defines a 'solution' as 'a means of solving a problem or dealing with a difficult situation'. This causes difficulty for solution-focused SST therapists who would rather deal with 'goals' than problems. As discussed in Chapter 22, a solution stands between a problem and a goal. Notwithstanding the preferred position of solution-focused therapists, a good solution in SST does have to render what the client regarded as a problem when they decided to seek therapy 'not a problem'. It also has to be considered as helping the client either to achieve their problem-related goal, or at least to take what is for them a significant step forward.

DOI: 10.4324/9781003413103-29

Given this, my definition of a solution in SST is as follows:

A solution in SST is a means by which a client renders their problem a 'non-problem' and/or deals effectively with an adversity. It also helps the client to achieve their problem-related goal or take a significant step towards achieving it.

This definition clearly favours SST therapists who work with problems *and* goals. For those who prefer to work with goals, I would put forward the following definition:

A solution in SST is a means by which a client achieves their goal or takes a significant step towards achieving it.

## The Chosen Solution and Potential Solutions

A solution tends to emerge from the part of the session where the therapist and client 'do the work'.[1] Given the focused nature of that work, the solutions that are available to the client within that context (called here 'potential' solutions) tend to be more limited than they were at the outset. For example, if somebody in Spain wants to visit a town in England and only has a day to do it, then they have a great many to choose from before they commit themself to fly into a particular airport. Once they make such a commitment, doing so limits their options.

Thus, it is significant for both client and therapist to realise that there are many potential solutions that could be chosen, and this becomes relevant if the work that the therapy dyad is doing is not progressing very well. When this happens, the therapist could say something like, 'It seems to me that what we are discussing here is not quite hitting the 'spot' concerning what you

---

1 As discussed in Chapter 24, this phrase is deliberately left vague so that SST therapists can practise in ways that they find effective. Remember, in SST there is no one way of 'doing the work'.

want to achieve. What do you think?' If the client agrees, then they can change tack, a decision that will probably result in a different range of potential solutions being considered. When the client selects a solution, it is known as a 'chosen' solution.

## The Importance of Negotiating a Solution

Whenever possible, the therapist and the client should negotiate a solution even if it is suggested by the therapist. Thus, family-oriented SST can involve one or two therapists working in the same room as the family with the session being observed by a team of therapists. At some point in the session, usually towards the end, a break is initiated by the therapist(s) to consult with the observing team out of the therapy room and from the resultant discussion an intervention is planned that generally involves a potential solution. However compelling this suggested solution might be, it still needs to be considered by the family, and it is possible that one or more family members may have difficulties with the solution. When this happens, the therapist(s) and family members discuss the matter until a solution that is acceptable to the family has been selected. Here, a negotiation has led to a chosen solution.

There are times, of course, when a therapy suggestion just hits the spot and this becomes the client's solution. From a working alliance perspective, the therapist and client are deemed to have agreed on the solution without any negotiation being necessary.

## Working Alliance Perspectives on Solutions

The concept of the working alliance can inform the SST therapist as they work with a client to select a solution. Thus, a good SST therapist helps their client to select a solution that:

- will help them to achieve their problem-related goal, if implemented;
- they have the skills and capability to execute;
- they have the confidence to execute or being willing to execute unconfidently until they gain confidence;
- has the therapeutic potency to enable the client to achieve their goal; and
- does not unwittingly serve to perpetuate their problem.

## Types of Solutions in SST

There are several types of solutions that the client can implement in SST. The selected solution should best meet the client's current situation.

*Environmental solutions.* An environmental solution involves the client changing or leaving an adverse situation that is unlikely to change.

*Behavioural solutions.* A behavioural solution involves the client changing their behaviour to solve their problem.

*Cognitive solutions.* A cognitive solution involves the client changing some aspect of their thinking about salient aspects of the problem. There are several different types of cognitive solution.

*Attitudinal change solutions.* An attitudinal change solution involves the client adopting a different evaluative stance towards the adversity.

*Inference change solutions.* An inference change solution involves the client changing a distorted inference that they have made about an adversity in the problematic situation.

*Reframe solutions.* A reframe solution involves the therapist helping the client put their problem in a new frame so that it is no longer a problem for them.

It is important to note that the above solutions can occur singly or in combination.

# Chapter 28

# Practising the Solution in the Session and Action Planning

## Abstract

In this chapter, I discuss the importance of the client practising their solution in the session (PSS). I discuss the reasons for doing so and not doing so and the forms that such practice may take. Once the client has finally decided on a solution to take forward, I discuss the importance of helping them to develop an action plan that will guide their implementation of the solution in their life and dealing with any obstacles to such implementation.

## Introduction

Once the client has selected a solution, and it has met the criteria of (i) potentially dealing with the problem and/or (ii) potentially achieving the problem-related goal or taking a significant step towards it, then ideally the next stage in the SST process is for the client to practise the solution in the session (PSS).

## Why PSS?

In my view, PSS helps the client answer one or more of the following questions.

DOI: 10.4324/9781003413103-30

### Does the Solution Feel Right?

PSS helps the client to get a better 'feel' for the solution. The selected solution may be the best solution for the client on paper, but, unless the client takes it out for a 'test run', they will not know, for certain, if it feels right enough for them to implement it in real life.

### Can the Client Make the Solution Work?

PSS helps the client to answer two questions: (i) 'Can I do it?' and (ii) 'Will it work?' Put more technically, such practice serves to help the client increase their efficacy expectations and outcome expectations, two cornerstones of self-efficacy theory originated by Bandura (1977).

### Does Anything about the Solution Need to Be Changed?

PSS helps the person determine whether or not anything about the solution needs to be modified. Hopefully, at this stage, this will involve the client in 'fine-tuning' the solution rather than making a radical overhaul.

### Does PSS Reveal Any Doubts, Reservations or Objections to the Solution?

Getting the experience of implementing the solution, albeit within the context of the therapy session, sometimes reveals to the client that they have a doubt, reservation or objection (DRO) to some aspect of the solution and its implementation. PSS gives the therapist and client an opportunity to identify and address any such DROs.

Given that the results of PSS need to be processed and discussed, the therapist needs to ensure that they structure the session in such a way that time is given to such processing and discussion.

While PSS helps the client to answer one or more of the above questions, perhaps its primary purpose is to give the client a success experience so that they can take the chosen solution home with them with optimism.

## Forms of PSS

While I will briefly list the main ways in which PSS can be carried out, I do wish to stress that this is an opportunity for both therapist and client to demonstrate their creativity in devising a way of implementing PSS. All relevant points discussed in the session and client variables identified in the pre-session form (or in the session if no such form was completed) are available to be incorporated into a PSS task.

### Behavioural Practice of a Behavioural Solution

Behavioural practice allows the client to practise a behavioural solution. For example, a client may have chosen assertion as their solution. Here the therapist might role-play the other person after being briefed by the client to put I into the role of the other.

### Behavioural Practice of a Cognitive Solution

Here, the client's actions help them to gain experience of their cognitive solution. An example of the latter is to be found in the work of Reinecke, Waldenmaier, Cooper and Harmer (2013). In their single-session treatment of panic, they gave clients a cognitive rationale of panic. This states that panic stems from a catastrophic misinterpretation of anxiety, which is maintained by the use of a range of safety-seeking manoeuvres and that 'terrible' things will rarely happen to a person if they allow themself to be anxious without using these safety-seeking manoeuvres. To practise this cognitive solution, 'I can allow myself to experience anxiety without using any safety-seeking manoeuvres', clients were given an immediate opportunity to rehearse this by practising it in a locked room. Such rehearsal proved to be a vital ingredient of the effectiveness of the single session. Here, the emphasis is on behavioural practice of a cognition solution in ways that are consistent with it. The client is not asked to engage in any deliberate rehearsal of any new cognition.

### Cognitive-Behavioural Practice of a Cognitive Solution

In CBT, the view is that the best way of changing an attitude is to think and act in ways that are consistent with the desired attitude. In PSS this is implemented by the client holding in mind the desired attitude while engaging in relevant behavioural practice. This practice differs for the previous practice in that, in this form, the client deliberately rehearses the new cognition while acting in ways that support it.

### Mental Rehearsal

Mental rehearsal involves the client picturing themself implementing the solution in their mind's eye. It is often referred to as imagery work. Here, the client can mentally rehearse any of the solutions mentioned above. They can do this to prepare themself to implement the solution in everyday life. I suggest that the client begins the mental rehearsal, picturing themself struggling and then developing competence through struggle. I do not suggest that they see themselves mastering the new solution as this is unrealistic.

### *Chairwork*

Scott Kellogg (2007: 8) says that:

> chairwork is a psychotherapeutic technique that typically involves the use of two chairs that face one another. The patient sits in one chair and has a dialogue with an imagined family member or other person sitting in the opposite chair; alternatively, the patient moves back and forth between the two chairs and speaks from different aspects of him- or herself.

There are four ways in which chairwork can be used in PSS (see Dryden, 2019a, Kellogg, 2015):

- promoting a dialogue with another person;
- promoting a dialogue between different parts of 'self';
- promoting a dialogue to correct a problem within 'self' (e.g. a problematic attitude); and
- role-playing.

Some solutions may not lend themselves to be practised in the session. For example, if the therapist has helped the client by encouraging them to reframe some aspect of their experience that led to the problem in the first place, this may be difficult to be rehearsed in the session. Even if it could be practised, doing so may interfere with the impact of the reframe. It is important to remember that, while it is generally a good thing for the client to practise their solution in the session, this is not universally the case.

Once the client has had an opportunity to practise their chosen solution in the session and has processed and discussed their experience with the therapist, both are ready to discuss how to implement the solution in the client's life.

## Helping the Client to Plan to Implement the Solution

When the client has finished practising the solution, and it has gone well, the therapist and client have a natural opportunity to discuss the client's plan to implement their solution when they need to in their everyday life. When discussing this, the client should be discouraged from adopting a waiting role concerning the adversity to which the client typically responds with their problematic response. Instead, they might be encouraged to seek out the adversity in order to implement the solution. For example, if the person has a problem with talking to people, rather than wait for someone to talk to them, they can practise their solution by initiating talking to a person.

In ongoing therapy, the therapist negotiates a specific 'homework' task with a client and then reviews it at the following session. This does not happen in SST. Instead, the therapist helps the client to develop a *general* plan to implement the solution and encourages them to find specific ways of implementing this plan going forward. This plan should contain some or all of the following features:

- the solution to be implemented;
- where the solution is to be implemented;
- when the solution is to be implemented;
- how often is the solution to be implemented; and
- if the solution is to be implemented with other people, these people should be specified in the plan.

It is important to recognise that the more the client can integrate the action plan into their everyday life, the more likely it is that they will be able to implement it.

### Identifying and Dealing with Potential Obstacles

After the action plan has been developed and guidelines for its implementation have been agreed upon, it is useful for the therapist to encourage the client to consider what obstacles they may encounter in carrying out the plan. Once a potential obstacle has been identified, it is the therapist's job to help their client to find the best way to address the obstacle so that it does not, in fact, stop them from implementing it. Once the therapist has done this, they can suggest an imagery exercise, where the client can be asked to imagine encountering the obstacle mentioned above and sees themself dealing with it constructively before picturing themself implementing the action plan.

Once the therapist has helped the client to develop an action plan and aided them in dealing with any obstacles to implementing the plan, then this is a sign that the ending phase of the session has been reached, and the therapist can begin the process of ending the session well, which is the topic of the next chapter.

# Chapter 29

# Bringing the Session to a Suitable End

## Abstract

In this chapter, I discuss three issues concerning the ending of the single session: (i) asking the client to summarise; (ii) agreeing on plans for future help and for follow-up; and (iii) tying up any loose ends.

## Introduction

As noted at the end of the previous chapter, after the therapist has helped the client to develop an action plan to practise the selected solution in their life and to identify and respond to any obstacles to its implementation, the ending phase of the session has been reached.[1]

## Asking the Client to Summarise

At some point during the ending phase of SST, it is useful for the client to summarise the session and what the client is going to take away with them. In SST, we suggest that the client summarises the session rather than the therapist because the client is going to take away points from their summary rather than from

---

1 See Hoyt & Rosenbaum (2018) for a more detailed discussion of how to end a session in SST.

DOI: 10.4324/9781003413103-31

the therapist's summary. My preference is for the client to summarise and I will prompt or add to the summary, if necessary. A good summary should contain (Dryden, 2019a):

- The client's problem and/or goal.
- The work done on the problem and/or towards the problem-related goal.
- What the client learned during this work and what they are going to takeaway.
- The solution the client selected and the strengths and resources they can draw on to deal with its implementation, and any obstacles identified and planned for.

Some therapists encourage their clients to make a written summary of what happened in the session, which features, in particular, what they learned and the chosen solution.

## Reviewing Options for Further Help

When the time has come to review the options for further help, the therapist needs to present them in an even-handed way. This means stressing that whichever option the client chooses is OK. Basically, there are three options with respect to further help. These should be outlined by the therapist as follows:

1. You may decide that you have got what you have come for and do not require further help at this time.
2. You may decide that you want the opportunity to (i) reflect on what you have learned; (ii) digest your learning, meaning that you will think about how to generalise your learning to other areas of your life; (iii) act on your learning; (iv) wait to see what happens before (v) you decide if you want further help.
   [In agencies that offer a OAATT service, meaning that, if the person wants more help, they can only access it one session at a time, there is usually a gap between the end of the

session and when the person can request further help. The intention is to encourage the client to engage in the 'reflect-digest-act-wait-decide process' described above. However, this does seem to penalise clients who know at the end of the first session that they need more help. Other agencies tell clients that they will call them in two or three weeks to see how they are doing and to see if they need more help.]

3. You may decide at the end of the session that you would like further help.

   [Here, the therapist needs to outline what services are available to the client together with waiting times before they can have their next appointment in the service they have selected.]

## Agreeing on a Follow-Up

Also, the therapist and client should agree on whether a follow-up session should be held and, if so, what the arrangements for that follow-up session should be. This will probably not apply to open-access, enter now SST. There will be more flexibility when SST is accessed with an independent practitioner than with an agency, which is likely to have a set policy concerning follow-up and when it is instituted. See Chapter 30 for a more detailed discussion of follow-ups.

## Tying Up Any Loose Ends

When the session ends, it is essential that the client leaves with a sense of completeness and optimism about the process. As such, the client should be invited to tell the therapist anything that they haven't mentioned that they need to say on the issue that they have been discussing before they leave the session. Also, if the client has any questions, they should be encouraged to ask them. Finally, if they have some DROs to any aspect of the process, they should be able to express them so that the therapist can respond. For example, the SST therapist could ask something like: 'If when you get home, you realise that you wished you could have asked me something or told me something, what might that be?' or 'Do you have any reservations about the work we did today that you would like to discuss with me before we finish today?' If a client goes away with an unasked and thus unanswered question or a reservation that has not been expressed and thus not dealt with, they may not get as much from the process as they otherwise could.

During this process, care should be taken not to invite the client to start talking about a new issue.

## Addendum

In my private practice, I offer the client the chance to have a digital voice recording (DVR) of the face-to-face session and a written transcript of the session.

I do this to help the client review what we discussed in the session and to reflect on and digest what they learned from the experience. It also happens that, when a client reviews the recording and transcript, they focus on an aspect of the session that they missed during the session itself that has significance for them. Clients, in particular, mention that they are pleased to have access to a summary of the session. Some make a copy of it and carry it around with them to review when necessary.

Some clients are pleased to have both the recording and the transcript, while others value one over the other. For example, some clients who do not like listening to their own voice prefer the transcript, while others who like listening to things 'on the go' on their smartphones favour the DVR. Given this, I provide clients with *both* the recording *and* the transcript[2] (Dryden, 2022a).

---

2 They do have to pay extra for the transcript. I charge them the sum that the professional transcriber charges me for the transcript.

Chapter 30

# Following-Through and Following-Up

## Abstract

In this final chapter, I consider issues concerning following-through and following-up. Following-through concerns what happens when a client decides to return and following-up concerns what happens when a client does not return, and the therapist wants to find out how they are doing and what their experience of SST was. As an example of the latter, I discuss how I follow-up with SST clients in my practice.

## Introduction

As stressed in Chapter 29, after a person leaves the session that may turn out to be the only session they need (or not), they should have a clear idea of whether or not they can return if they need further help and how they can access that help.

## Following-Through

Following-through occurs when the client returns for more help.[1] When a client requests another single session then the therapist should aim to see them very quickly to preserve the

---

1 Here I will focus on the situation where the client returns for another single session.

DOI: 10.4324/9781003413103-32

'help at the point of need' principle that underpins SST (see Chapter 4). When the client is seen, the therapist should ensure that there is continuity between the first SST session and the second. When the returning client is struggling with the problem for which they first sought help, the therapist should find out what their experiences were of implementing the solution that the client chose. In particular, what was helpful when they did so and what did not help. Also, the therapist should find out which internal strengths and external resources the client made use of in implementing the solution and which could have been drawn upon, but were not.

The therapist is advised to discover (i) whether the client needs help to retain the original solution and change some aspects of it and perhaps use internal strengths and external resources that they could have used but did not do so or (ii) whether they need to select and be helped to implement a different solution. If the former is the case, after the modifications have been decided upon, the client should be invited to practise it in the session, as outlined in Chapter 28. If the latter is the case, then the session will resemble the first session. Indeed, in such circumstances, it may be useful for the therapist to start from scratch unless it is clear why the solution did not work, in which case the new session can be built on such understanding. When a new solution has been chosen by the client, once again they should be invited to practise it in the session and action planning should be done. If the new solution does not yield a better outcome, the client may return for another session. If this pattern continues, then, if a different therapy service is available (e.g. a block of sessions or ongoing therapy), the therapist and client may decide that it is better for the client to access a different form of help.

## Following-Up

Following-up occurs when the client has not requested more help after the single session. The follow-up session occurs at a time agreed by the therapist and client and typically takes place months rather than weeks after the single session. There are a few people in the single-session community who think that a follow-up session is not a part of SST, which they define as one session and one session only. Most people, however, consider that a follow-up session is an integral part of SST.

## Why Follow Up?

A follow-up session provides information on outcome, the client's view of the session and, if relevant, the client' view of the service in which SST took place.

## My Approach to Follow-Up

As an example of follow-up in SST, let me outline my approach to this issue (Dryden, 2022a). At the end of the session, I make a specific arrangement for a follow-up phone call that lasts between 20 and 30 minutes. The client and I agree on a date, which is usually about three months after the session to enable any changes the client has made to mature and be incorporated into their life. I stress that it is crucial for the session to be scheduled at a time and place where the client can talk free from distraction and interruption. I want the client to give me their full attention. Here is the framework I use in the follow-up session.

### Outcome

I first inquire about matters to do with the outcome of the session. I begin by stating the reason why the client came for help originally.

- Has the issue changed (for better or worse or has there been no change)?
- What brought about the change or what made the problem stay the same?

- Have others noticed any change? If so, what have they noticed?
- Have other areas of your life changed for better or worse?

### The session

I then ask about the client's experience of the session itself.

- What do you recall from the therapy session you had?
- What was particularly helpful or unhelpful?
- What use did you make of the session recording and transcript?
- How satisfied are you with the therapy that you received?
- Did you find the single session to be sufficient? If not, would you wish to resume therapy? If so, would you like to see another therapist?
- If you had any recommendations for improvement in the service that you received, what would they be?

### Other

The final question I ask is as follows.

- Is there anything else I have not specifically asked you that you would like me to know?

This brings us to the end of this book. I hope that you have found it valuable. I would welcome any feedback that you have for me. Please send an email to windy@windydryden.com.

# References

Appelbaum, S.A. (1975). Parkinson's Law in psychotherapy. *International Journal of Psychoanalytic Psychotherapy, 4*, 426–436.

Bandura, A. (1977). Self-efficacy: Toward a unifying theory of behavioral change. *Psychological Review, 84*, 191–215.

Barkham, M., & Lambert, M.J. (2021). The efficacy and effectiveness of psychological therapies. In M. Barkham, W. Lutz & L.G. Castonguay (Eds.), *Bergin and Garfield's Handbook of Psychotherapy and Behavior Change.* 50th anniversary edition. (pp. 115–189). Hoboken, NJ: Wiley.

Battino, R. (2014). Expectation: The essence of very brief therapy. In M.F. Hoyt & M. Talmon (Eds.), *Capturing the Moment: Single Session Therapy and Walk-In Services* (pp. 393–406). Bethel, CT: Crown House Publishing.

Bloom, B.L. (1981). Focused single-session therapy: Initial development and evaluation. In S. Budman (Ed.), *Forms of Brief Therapy* (pp. 167–216). New York: Guilford Press.

Bloom, B.L. (1992). *Planned Short-Term Psychotherapy: A Clinical Handbook.* Boston, MA: Allyn and Bacon.

Bordin, E.S. (1979). The generalizability of the psychoanalytic concept of the working alliance. *Psychotherapy: Theory, Research and Practice, 16*, 252–260.

Boscolo, L., Cecchin, G., Hoffman, L., & Penn, P. (1987). *Milan Systemic Family Therapy.* New York: Basic Books.

Constantino, M.J., Ametrano, R.M., & Greenberg, R.P. (2012). Clinician interventions and participant characteristics that foster adaptive patient expectations for psychotherapy and psychotherapeutic change. *Psychotherapy, 49*, 557–569.

Constantino, M.J., Glass, C.R., Arnkoff, D.B., Ametrano, R.M., & Smith, J.Z. (2011). Expectations. In J.C. Norcross (Ed.), *Psychotherapy Relationships that Work: Evidence-Based Responsiveness* (2nd ed.; pp. 354–376). New York: Oxford University Press.

Cummings, N.A. (1990). Brief intermittent psychotherapy through the life cycle. In J.K. Zeig & S.G. Gilligan (Eds.), *Brief Therapy: Myths, Methods and Metaphors* (pp. 169–194). New York: Brunner/Mazel.

De Shazer, S. (1982). *Patterns of Brief Family Therapy.* New York: Guilford Press.

Dryden, W. (2006). *Counselling in a Nutshell.* London: Sage.

Dryden, W. (2011). *Counselling in a Nutshell* (2nd ed.). London: Sage.

Dryden, W. (2016). *When Time Is At a Premium: Cognitive-Behavioural Approaches to Single-Session Therapy and Very Brief Coaching.* London: Rationality Publications.

Dryden, W. (2018a). *Very Brief Therapeutic Conversations.* Abingdon: Routledge.

Dryden, W. (2018b). From problems to goals. Identifying 'good' goals in counselling and psychotherapy. In M. Cooper & D. Law (Eds.), *Working with Goals in Counselling and Psychotherapy* (pp. 139–159). Oxford: Oxford University Press.

Dryden, W. (2019a). *Single-Session Therapy: 100 Key Points and Techniques.* Abingdon: Routledge.

Dryden, W. (2019b). *The Relevance of Rational Emotive Behaviour Therapy for Modern CBT and Psychotherapy.* Abingdon: Routledge.

Dryden, W. (2022a). *Single-Session Integrated CBT (SSI-CBT): Distinctive Features* (2nd ed.). Abingdon: Routledge.

Dryden, W. (2022b). *Single-Session Therapy: Responses to Frequently Asked Questions.* Abingdon: Routledge.

Dryden, W. (2023). *ONEplus Therapy: Help at the Point of Need.* Sheffield: Onlinevents.

Dryden, W. (2024). *Single-Session Therapy: 100 Key Points and Techniques.* 2nd edition. Abingdon: Routledge.

Ellis, A., & Joffe, D. (2002). A study of volunteer clients who experienced live sessions of rational emotive behavior therapy in front of a public audience. *Journal of Rational-Emotive & Cognitive-Behavior Therapy, 20,* 151–158.

Findlay, R. (2007). A mandate for honesty, Jeff Young's No Bullshit Therapy: An interview. *Australian and New Zealand Journal of Family Therapy, 28* (3), 165–170.

Freud, S., & Breuer, J. (1895). *Studien Über Hysterie*. Leipzig: Deuticke.

Garfield, S.L. (1995). *Psychotherapy: An Eclectic-Integrative Approach* (2nd ed.). New York: John Wiley & Sons.

Gonzalez, M.T., Estrada, B., & O'Hanlon, B. (2011). Possibilities and solutions: The differences that make a difference. *International Journal of Hispanic Psychology, 3* (2), 185–200.

Goulding, M.M., & Goulding, R.L. (1979). *Changing Lives through Redecision Therapy*. New York: Grove Press.

Haley, J. (1989). *The First Therapy Session: How to Interview Clients and Identify Problems Successfully* (audiotape). San Francisco, CA: Jossey-Bass.

Hayes, A.M., Laurenceau, J-P., Feldman, G., Strauss, J.L., & Cardaciotto, L. (2007). Change is not always linear: The study of nonlinear and discontinuous patterns of change in psychotherapy. *Clinical Psychology Review, 27*, 715–723.

Hoyt, M.F. (1990). On time in brief therapy. In R.A. Wells & V.J. Gianetti (Eds.), *Handbook of the Brief Psychotherapies* (pp. 115–143). New York: Plenum.

Hoyt, M.F. (2000). *Some Stories Are Better than Others: Doing What Works in Brief Therapy and Managed Care*. Philadelphia, PA: Brunner/Mazel.

Hoyt, M.F. (2011). Foreword. In A. Slive & M. Bobele (Eds.), *When One Hour Is All You Have: Effective Therapy for Walk-in Clients* (pp. xix–xv). Phoenix, AZ: Zeig, Tucker, & Theisen.

Hoyt, M.F. (2018). Single-session therapy: Stories, structures, themes, cautions, and prospects. In M.F. Hoyt, M. Bobele, A. Slive, J. Young, & M. Talmon (Eds.), *Single-Session Therapy by Walk-In or Appointment: Administrative, Clinical, and Supervisory Aspects of One-at-a-Time Services* (pp. 155–174). New York: Routledge.

Hoyt, M.F., & Rosenbaum, R. (2018). Some ways to end an SST. In M.F. Hoyt, M. Bobele, A. Slive, J. Young, & M. Talmon (Eds.), *Single-Session Therapy by Walk-In or Appointment: Administrative, Clinical, and Supervisory Aspects of One-at-a-Time Services* (pp. 318–323). New York: Routledge.

Hoyt, M.F., & Talmon, M.F. (Eds.). (2014a). *Capturing the Moment: Single Session Therapy and Walk-In Services*. Bethel, CT: Crown House Publishing.

Hoyt, M.F., & Talmon, M.F. (2014b). What the literature says: An annotated bibliography. In M.F. Hoyt & M. Talmon (Eds.), *Capturing the*

*Moment: Single Session Therapy and Walk-In Services* (pp. 487–516). Bethel, CT: Crown House Publishing.

Hoyt, M.F., Bobele, M., Slive, A., Young, J., & Talmon, M. (Eds.). (2018a). *Single-Session Therapy by Walk-In or Appointment: Administrative, Clinical, and Supervisory Aspects of One-at-a-Time Services.* New York: Routledge.

Hoyt, M.F., Bobele, M., Slive, A., Young, J., & Talmon, M. (2018b). Single-session/one-at-a-time walk-in therapy. In M.F. Hoyt, M. Bobele, A. Slive, J. Young, & M. Talmon (Eds.), *Single-Session Therapy by Walk-In or Appointment: Administrative, Clinical, and Supervisory Aspects of One-at-a-Time Services* (pp. 3–24). New York: Routledge.

Hoyt, M.F., Young, J., & Rycroft, P. (Eds.). (2021). *Single Session Thinking and Practice in Global, Cultural and Familial Contexts: Expanding Applications.* New York: Routledge.

Iveson, C., George, E., & Ratner, H. (2014). Love is all around: A single session solution-focused therapy. In M.F. Hoyt & M. Talmon (Eds.), *Capturing the Moment: Single Session Therapy and Walk-In Services* (pp. 325–348). Bethel, CT: Crown House Publishing.

Jacobson, N.S., Follette, W.C., & Revenstorf, D. (1984). Psychotherapy outcome research: Methods for reporting variability and evaluating clinical significance. *Behavior Therapy, 15,* 336–352.

Kellogg, S.H. (2007). Transformational chairwork: Five ways of using therapeutic dialogues. *NYSPA Notebook, 19* (4), 8–9.

Kellogg, S.H. (2015). *Transformational Chairwork: Using Psychotherapeutic Dialogues in Clinical Practice.* Lanham, MD: Rowman & Littlefield.

Kuehn, J.L. (1965). Encounter at Leyden: Gustav Mahler consults Sigmund Freud. *Psychoanalytic Review, 52,* 345–364.

Lonergan, J. (2012, Autumn). 'I alone must do it, but I cannot do it alone'. *Inside Out,* Issue 68. [http://iahip.org/inside-out/issue-68-autumn-2012/i-alone-must-do-it-but-i-cannot-do-it-alone-a-talk-by-john-lonergan-a-decade-on-10th-anniversary-celebration-of-inside-out] (accessed 7 November 2018).

McElheran, N., Stewart, J., Soenen, D., Newman, J., & MacLaurin, B. (2014). Walk-in single session therapy at the Eastside Family Centre. In M.F. Hoyt & M. Talmon (Eds.), *Capturing the Moment: Single Session Therapy and Walk-In Services* (pp. 177–195). Bethel, CT: Crown House Publishing.

Miller, W.R., & C'de Baca, J. (2001). *Quantum Change: When Epiphanies and Sudden Insights Transform Ordinary Lives*. New York: Guilford.

Norcross, J.C., & Cooper, M. (2021). *Personalizing Psychotherapy: Assessing and Accommodating Patient Preferences.* Washington, DC: American Psychological Association.

O'Hanlon, B. (1999). *Do One Thing Different: And Other Uncommonly Sensible Solutions to Life's Persistent Problems.* New York: W. Morrow & Co.

O'Hanlon, W.H., & Hexum, A.L. (1990). *An Uncommon Casebook: The Complete Clinical Work of Milton H. Erickson M.D.* New York: Norton.

Paul, K.E., & van Ommeren, P. (2013). A primer on single session therapy and its potential application in humanitarian situations. *Intervention, 11* (1), 8–23.

Pitman, J. (2017). *The Invisible Man: The Story of Rod Temperton, the 'Thriller' Songwriter*. Stroud: The History Press.

Ratner, H., George, E., & Iveson, C. (2012). *Solution Focused Brief Therapy: 100 Key Points and Techniques*. Hove: Routledge.

Reinecke, A., Waldenmaier, L., Cooper, M.J., & Harmer, C.J. (2013). Changes in automatic threat processing precede and predict clinical changes with exposure-based cognitive-behavior therapy for panic disorder. *Biological Psychiatry, 73*, 1064–1070.

Rogers, C.R. (1957). The necessary and sufficient conditions of therapeutic personality change. *Journal of Consulting Psychology, 21*, 95–103.

Rosenthal, R., & Jacobson, L. (1968). *Pygmalion in the Classroom: Teacher Expectation and Pupils' Intellectual Development*. New York: Holt, Rinehart & Winston.

Seabury, B.A., Seabury, B.H., & Garvin, C.D. (2011). *Foundations of Interpersonal Practice in Social Work: Promoting Competence in Generalist Practice.* 3rd ed. Thousand Oaks, CA: Sage Publications.

Sharoff, K. (2002). *Cognitive Coping Therapy*. New York: Brunner-Mazel.

Simon, G.E., Imel, Z.E., Ludman, E.J., & Steinfeld, B.J. (2012). Is dropout after a first psychotherapy visit always a bad outcome? *Psychiatric Services, 63* (7), 705–707.

Talmon, M. (1990). *Single Session Therapy: Maximising the Effect of the First (and Often Only) Therapeutic Encounter*. San Francisco, CA: Jossey-Bass.

Talmon, M. (1993). *Single Session Solutions: A Guide to Practical, Effective and Affordable Therapy*. New York: Addison-Wesley.

Talmon, M. (2018). The eternal now: On becoming and being a single-session therapist. In M.F. Hoyt, M. Bobele, A. Slive, J. Young, & M. Talmon (Eds.), *Single-Session Therapy by Walk-In or Appointment: Administrative, Clinical, and Supervisory Aspects of One-at-a Time Services* (pp. 149–154). New York: Routledge.

Young, J. (2018). SST: The misunderstood gift that keeps on giving. In M.F. Hoyt, M. Bobele, A. Slive, J. Young, & M. Talmon (Eds.), *Single-Session Therapy by Walk-In or Appointment: Administrative, Clinical, and Supervisory Aspects of One-at-a-Time Services* (pp. 40–58). New York: Routledge.

# 30 Ideas That Inform My Practice of Single-Session Therapy

## General Ideas

- Making an emotional impact
- Using humour
- Utilising the 'user manual' approach[1]
- Helping the client to respond to their initial reactions
- Using the book analogy[2]
- Helping the client to determine whether they have solved the problem before
- Helping the client to understand the problem before suggesting 'tips and techniques'
- Helping the client to develop confidence by doing things unconfidently
- Helping the client to view discomfort as a friend and not as an enemy
- Helping the client distinguish between enthusiasm-based motivation, fear-based motivation and reason-based motivation

---

1 By 'user manual', I mean a notional way of understanding how a unique person 'works' and using that information to improve one's relationship with self and others.
2 The 'book analogy' recognises that, after an adversity happens in Chapter 1, there are other chapters in the book that follow where the person can deal productively with this adversity.

## REBT-Informed Ideas

- Helping the client to distinguish between unhealthy and healthy negative emotions
- Getting to the heart of the matter[3]
- Encouraging the client to develop a flexible attitude
- Helping the client to develop an attitude of bearability
- Helping the client to take the horror out of badness
- Helping the client to develop an attitude of unconditional self-acceptance
- Helping the client to develop an attitude of unconditional other-acceptance
- Helping the client to accept reality
- Using Windy's Review Assessment Procedure (WRAP)[4]
- Helping clients to examine their attitudes
- Helping the client to understand and deal with anxiety
- Helping the client to understand and deal with depression
- Helping the client to understand and deal with guilt
- Helping the client to understand and deal with unhealthy regret
- Helping the client to understand and deal with shame
- Helping the client to understand and deal with unhealthy anger
- Helping the client to understand and deal with hurt
- Helping the client to understand and deal with unhealthy jealousy
- Helping the client to understand and deal with unhealthy envy
- Helping the client to understand and deal with procrastination

3 This involves helping the client to identify the adversity that lies at the heart of their problem.
4 This is a quick way to help a client identify the unhelpful attitudes that underpin their pin their problems and their healthy attitudinal alternatives.

# What Is ONEplus Therapy

Information for Prospective Clients
Windy Dryden, PhD

- ONEplus Therapy[1] is an intentional endeavour where you and I set out with the purpose of helping you in one session, on the understanding that more help is available to you if you want it.
- At the end of the session, we will agree on a way forward. Thus, (i) you may decide to seek no further help; (ii) you may decide to reflect on and digest what you learned in the session, act on what you learned and see what happens before deciding whether to seek further help; or (iii) you may decide to arrange for further help at the end of the session. If the latter, we can discuss what further help is available so you can choose what best suits you. Each of these ways forward is equally OK.
- ONEplus Therapy is based on offering help at the point of need rather than at the point of availability. It has the effect of you being seen quickly when you need help.
- ONEplus Therapy is based on three foundations:

---

1 See Chapter 1 for a brief explanation concerning why I call my SST work ONEplus therapy.

- The most frequent number of sessions clients have internationally is '1', followed by '2', '3', and so on.
- 70–80% of those who have one session are satisfied with that session, given their current circumstances.
- Therapists are poor at predicting who will attend only one session and who will attend more.
- My primary goal in ONEplus Therapy is to provide you with the help YOU want. This may include me:
  - Helping you to address a specific issue with which you are stuck. Here I will help you to take a few steps forward, which may encourage you to travel the rest of the journey without my professional assistance.
  - Helping you to get a greater understanding of an issue.
  - Helping you to express your feelings about an issue.
  - Helping you to make a decision or resolve a dilemma.
- People have found it helpful to prepare for the session so that they can get the most from it. To this end, I will send you a questionnaire to complete and return. This is NOT compulsory, but it helps us both prepare for the session.
- The focus of a session in ONEplus Therapy is on us negotiating a goal for that session. If you have a specific issue that you wish to address, I will help you to find and rehearse a solution that facilitates the achievement of this goal. Then, I will help you to devise an action plan that you can implement after the session.
- In ONEplus Therapy, I will help you to:
  - Discover what you have done in the past to deal with your problem. I will then encourage you to use what has been helpful and set aside what has not been helpful.
  - Identify and use your internal strengths and external resources in implementing the agreed solution.
- I encourage follow-up to discover how you are getting on and to improve service delivery, and at the end of the session we will make an appointment for a follow-up, but only if you wish.

# Therapeutic Contract with Professor Windy Dryden

## ONEplus Therapy

Here are the elements of my practice that you need to know and agree with before you become a client of mine.

1. We will meet either face-to-face or online by Zoom. At the moment, I am only offering Zoom sessions.
2. If we are meeting online by Zoom, I will send you a link in advance.
3. All our meetings are confidential with the exception of the following:
   a. If you are at risk to yourself and are not prepared to take steps to protect your life or well-being, I will take steps to protect you in these respects.
   b. If you pose a risk to others and are not prepared to take steps to protect them, I will take steps to protect them from you.
   c. I am professionally mandated to report past or present incidents of child abuse that have not previously been reported.
   d. If I am formally requested to hand over my notes to the courts then I am obliged to do so.
4. I will not speak or correspond with others about you without your formal, written permission. If anybody contacts me about you and I do not have your written authority to speak

or correspond with them, then I will not do so and will inform you about this.

5. I have a 48-hour cancellation policy. I will charge you if you do not give me the full 48-hour notice that you wish to cancel your appointment. If I do not give you full 48-hour notice if I need to cancel our appointment, then you do not pay for the rearranged session. The exception is if either you, I, or one of our loved ones has to be hospitalised.

6. Before the session, I will send you a pre-session questionnaire for you to complete and return. The form's primary purpose is to help you get the most from the session.

7. My fee is £XXX per session (up to 50-minute session), payable in advance by BACS. This fee includes my processing of your pre-session questionnaire, the session and the audio-recording of the session.

8. If you want a transcript of the session, this will be £XX extra. Please tell me whether or not you want this transcript.

9. If we agree to a follow-up appointment, there will be an extra charge depending on what type of follow-up we decide to have.

Please confirm that you agree with these conditions by signing and dating a copy of this form and returning it to me.

I have read the above and agree with the conditions stated.

Signed............................................

Date..............................................

# Index

Printed in the United States
by Baker & Taylor Publisher Services